Facebook

Leverage Social Media to Grow Your Business

Marketing

Steven Holzner

800 East 96th Street, Indianapolis, Indiana 46240 USA

Facebook Marketing: Leverage Social Media to Grow Your Business

Copyright © 2009 by Que Publishing

ISBN-13: 978-0-789-73802-8
ISBN-10: 0-7897-3802-3

Library of Congress Cataloging-in-Publication Data:

Holzner, Steven.
  Facebook marketing : leverage social media to grow your business / Steven Holzner.
    p. cm.
  Includes index.
  ISBN 978-0-7897-3802-8
  1. Internet marketing. 2. Internet advertising. 3. Facebook. 4. Social networks—Computer network resources. 5. Internet marketing—Case studies. I. Title.
  HF5415.1265.H656 2009
  658.8'72—dc22
                    2008033866

Printed in the United States of America

First Printing September 2008

Trademarks

Warning and Disclaimer

Bulk Sales

Que Publishing offers excellent discounts on this book when ordered in quantity for bulk purchases or special sales. For more information, please contact:

U.S. Corporate and Government Sales

1-800-382-3419

corpsales@pearsontechgroup.com

For sales outside of the U.S., please contact:

International Sales

international@pearson.com

Associate Publisher
Greg Wiegand

Acquisitions Editor
Loretta Yates

Development Editor
Kevin Howard

Managing Editor
Kristy Hart

Project Editor
Chelsey Marti

Copy Editor
Gayle Johnson

Indexer
Erika Millen

Proofreader
Leslie Joseph

Technical Editor
Chris Treadaway

Publishing Coordinator
Cindy Teeters

Cover Designer
Anne Jones

Composition
Nonie Ratcliff

Contents at a Glance

Contents

About the Author

Steven Holzner is the award-winning author of 112 books and has been a contributing editor at *PC Magazine*. His books have sold three million copies and have been translated into 18 languages. He specializes in web topics such as Facebook. He has been marketing his own companies on the Web for years, using marketplace experience; banner ads; Google, Yahoo!, and MSN pay-per-click campaigns; viral marketing; Usenet marketing; and more. He's a web entrepreneur and has three online companies, which keep him busy.

Dedication

To Nancy, of course.

Acknowledgments

This book is the work of many people. I'd particularly like to thank Loretta Yates, Kevin Howard, Chris Treadaway, and Chelsey Marti.

We Want to Hear from You!

As the reader of this book, *you* are our most important critic and commentator. We value your opinion, and we want to know what we're doing right, what we could do better, what areas you'd like to see us publish in, and any other words of wisdom you're willing to pass our way.

You can email or write me directly to let me know what you did or didn't like about this book—as well as what we can do to make our books stronger.

Please note that I cannot help you with technical problems related to the topic of this book, and that due to the high volume of mail I receive, I might not be able to reply to every message.

When you write, please be sure to include this book's title and author as well as your name and phone number or email address. I will carefully review your comments and share them with the author and editors who worked on the book.

Email: greg.wiegand@pearson.com

Mail: Greg Wiegand
        Associate Publisher
        Que Publishing
        800 East 96th Street
        Indianapolis, IN 46240 USA

Reader Services

Visit our website and register this book at informit.com/register for convenient access to any updates, downloads, or errata that might be available for this book.

Introduction

Facebook has 42 million users, and they're smart, affluent, Internet-savvy people whom marketers can no longer ignore.

However, traditional marketing methods won't work here. In Facebook, the users are in charge, not the marketers, and that's a fact we have to live with.

Facebook members can comment on your brand, and there's not much you can do about it. The marketing channel is reversed—rather than top-down, things now move from the bottom up. Now that your customers can talk back, for good or ill, it pays to listen to what they have to say.

Learning to live with the new rules of social marketing is what this book is all about. If you want to survive and thrive in this world, you have to provide content, not just ad copy. Rather than interruptive advertising, you have to go viral. And spam can get you kicked out.

Facebook has tons of profit potential. Facebook users are not averse to marketing—they're just averse to unilateral marketing that feels like marketing.

What's in This Book

This book is a survey of Facebook and where marketers fit in. Facebook has many nooks and crannies that aren't obvious to the casual user, and ferreting them out can be tough. Here's what's in this book:

Chapter 1, "Targeting Your Profile"

Most social interaction on Facebook revolves around your profile, and this chapter is all about setting up this most basic of Facebook tools. You'll learn about the various sections of the Facebook profile, which is essential knowledge for the rest of the book.

Chapter 2, "Facebook Groups"

Facebook groups allow Facebook members to congregate and discuss issues—including your brand. Users can post text items, photos, and videos and hold discussions. This chapter shows you how to use groups and create your own group.

Chapter 3, "Creating Your Own Pages"

People have profiles on Facebook. Brands, bands, and companies have Facebook pages, which are much like profiles. Facebook members don't become friends of a page, however; they become fans. This chapter shows you how Facebook pages work, as well as how to create your own Facebook page.

Chapter 4, "Hosting Your Own Facebook Events"

Facebook events are, as their name implies, pages about one-time events that you want people to know about. For example, your store could be having a big sale, a company picnic, or a sponsored event, such as a music event. This chapter shows you how to get the word out.

Chapter 5, "Introducing Advertising"

Facebook now allows ads (it didn't used to). These can be displayed in various places, and you can pay using cost per click or cost per impression. Social ads tie into the actions that users perform on Facebook. We'll explore all the options in this chapter.

Chapter 6, "Optimizing and Monitoring Your Advertising"

Having spent money on advertising, you'd like to know how effective those ads are—what your click-through ratio is, how many impressions you're getting, and so on. Facebook recently added ad analytics, and they're improving all the time, so we'll take a look in this chapter.

Chapter 7, "Using the Marketplace"

If you have items to sell, Facebook is up to the task with its marketplace. You can list items for sale here, and people can get in touch with you about them. In other words, the marketplace is Facebook's classified section. It's free, and it works, and it can be useful to some marketers.

Chapter 8, "Beacon, Polls, and Networks"

Chapter 8 discusses some more-advanced marketing techniques—Beacon, polls, and handling networks.

Beacon is Facebook's effort to "Facebookize" the entire Web for the benefit of marketers. Using Beacon, sites around the Web can add Facebook users' actions on their sites to the news feeds on Facebook (for example, "Ethmoid Studge bought a book on booksbooks-booksetc.com") and include a link. Because the news feed is the chief way that marketing goes viral on Facebook, that can be pretty powerful.

Facebook polls allow you to ask your potential customers questions and get immediate results. Polls are displayed in users' news feeds, and users seem to have no problem letting their voices be heard—which is a great marketing tool.

As you'll see in this book, much of Facebook centers on what network(s) you belong to. You'll discover how to use this to your advantage—such as by posting on the network pages, which is where Facebook comes the closest to tolerating outright spam. You'll also see how to suggest a new network to Facebook.

Chapter 9, "Facebook Applications"

Facebook has recently been thrown open to third-party developers, who create applications that can be displayed in users' profiles and pages. There are many ways for marketers to take advantage of this. Many applications can display advertising, and you can buy space in them, using various ad networks. You can also use many applications to further your social networking on Facebook. And finally, you can hire developers to build your own applications, dedicated to your brand. You'll see all of that in this chapter.

Chapter 10, "Developing Your Own Applications"

The last chapter gives you an overview of what's involved in creating your own Facebook applications. You'll build an actual Facebook application and get it running. And you'll explore—and get working—various calls to the Facebook API.

What You'll Need

All you need in this book is a Facebook account. So if you don't already have one, go to http://www.facebook.com and sign up. As soon as you're on Facebook, you're ready to turn to Chapter 1.

Targeting Your Profile

In This Chapter:

- Welcome to Facebook Marketing
- Signing Up for Facebook
- Understanding Your Profile
- An Overview of Facebook

"[In] the last hundred years…the way to advertise was to get into the mass media and push out your content…In the next hundred years information won't be just pushed out to people, it will be shared among the millions of connections people have. Advertising will change. You will need to get into these connections."

Mark Zuckerberg
CEO Facebook

Welcome to Facebook Marketing

Welcome to Facebook—a premiere social networking site, meeting place for about 80 million users, and marketer's dream—if you know how to market there. We want to say from the outset that the old marketing standby, interruption marketing, in which the viewer has to sit through an ad, won't cut it on Facebook. We're into a whole new realm of marketing now, with new terms such as content marketing and viral marketing.

It's a new world for marketers, who are just coming to grips with that new world. The potential is enormous, and the payoff is huge—if you play by the Facebook community's rules. It's not as though marketing is imposed on Facebook users who don't want to see it. Most Facebook users are interested in what you have to offer, if you present it effectively—and correctly.

That's what this book is all about—the marketing revolution that is social networking. Contrary to what you may have heard, marketing is not an anathema in social networking—far from it. But marketers have a steep learning curve.

This book penetrates the world of social networking from a marketer's perspective. Again, let me emphasize that marketing is not at all unwelcome on Facebook, but it can't look like standard, old-world marketing.

This book shows you what works and what to avoid. The main difference between old-world and new-world marketing is that now your potential customers are much more in control of their environment, and you're the one who has to fit in. Unlike the passive consumers targeted by television advertising, Facebook users can talk to each other, form groups, and polarize for or against what you have to offer.

It's no longer the corporation with the biggest budget that wins. Stunning marketing upsets are occurring in the social networks every day. Your creativity—and your ability to engage users—determine your success.

That's a fundamental change: your potential customers are now in charge of the marketing environment, and you must be the one who fits in, not the reverse. Yet the rewards are immense, so it's worth your while to understand the new rules. It's a matter of watching and learning, so we'll look at what works and what doesn't, at case studies, at interviews with marketers, and more.

Dozens of tools are available to marketers on Facebook, but you have to be careful. If you screw up, or try to bludgeon your potential customers with your message, you will be dead in the water. Either you'll be ostracized, or Facebook will remove your account for spamming.

This chapter introduces the basics of Facebook—topics and resources we'll take for granted in the coming chapters, such as Facebook profiles, the Wall, friends, and more. In other words, this chapter lays the foundation for the rest of the book.

If you're already an accomplished Facebook user, you might want to skip to Chapter 2, "Facebook Groups." Otherwise, let's begin with an overview of Facebook.

Welcome to Facebook

Facebook has about 80 million users. This is smaller than the biggest social networking site, MySpace (a whopping 200 million registered users), but bigger than the business-contact-oriented LinkedIn (about 20 million or so).

Even though it's not the biggest, I believe that Facebook provides the best opportunity for marketers. LinkedIn has a reputation for being primarily for the over-35 group, and people there are interested in their careers; they aren't as concerned with socializing. It's not a site you spend hours on; it's more of a business environment.

And, for my taste, MySpace is too chaotic and coarse to provide a fruitful environment for marketers. MySpace has the registered users, but the pages can be so hard to deal with that, unlike Facebook, I don't feel like browsing people on MySpace. People tend to spend much more time on Facebook than they do on MySpace.

The Facebook demographics are the most opportune for marketers. Facebook started on February 4, 2004 (MySpace started in August 2003 and LinkedIn in May 2003) as a site for college students. You had to have a college email address (ending in .edu) to join.

That changed in September 2006. Then anyone with a valid email address could join, but from a marketer's point of view, Facebook's beginnings were crucial. It still has the reputation of being upscale compared to MySpace, and the typical user is still college-age—with plenty of disposable income.

MySpace is a zoo that screams at you from the page, and LinkedIn is a reserved, formal world of business contacts. Facebook is home to an extremely desirable demographic—educated 18-to-26-year-olds—and it's where they feel comfortable. It's where they live with their friends online, and it's where you usually have the best chance of marketing.

What's the attraction of Facebook? What draws people and keeps them there hour after hour?

In a word: friends. That's what social networking is all about. And Facebook excels at connecting users with friends and keeping them in touch. That's a vital need for many college students—not only while they're in school, but after they leave. For that reason, you'll see the average demographic on Facebook age as time goes on.

Not only can you add other users as your friends, which gives them access to your information, you also can stay in touch with them. You can drop by their pages and leave them notes on "the Wall," as we'll see in this chapter. You can send them messages. (For some reason, many Facebook users treat Facebook messages as more handy than standard email.) You can tell them about events you've registered with Facebook.

Even better—and this is the truly valuable part, and one of the main draws of Facebook—you can watch what your friends are doing minute by minute. Facebook watches your friends' activities and reports them to you (consistent with the level of privacy that your friends have set). So you can see what your friends are up to as they perform Facebook actions.

This is one of the main ways that Facebook forms its cohesive community—by keeping you in touch with what your friends are doing without any special action on their part. It's a sort of proximity-by-proxy thing, and it's the closest that two people in different states might come to staying in touch. For that reason, many Facebook users keep a Facebook window open at all times when they're doing other work on their computer—to watch their friends.

You can also give your status on Facebook, and anyone can see what you're doing. For example, you can list yourself as online, as working, as having fun—whatever.

From the users' point of view, Facebook is really all about connecting with your friends. In fact, Facebook offers suggestions on your Friends page, listing Facebook members you may already know. It finds these people by checking what networks you've joined and what friends you may have in common with other users.

If this chapter's overview of Facebook leaves you feeling lost, take a look at a good introductory book on Facebook, because the rest of this book takes the basics for granted.

What insightful pieces of advice would you most want new marketers on Facebook to know?

Be as authentic in your marketing as possible. Inside social networks, trusted referrals are the most powerful marketing message. Find ways to expose your target audience to people who authentically evangelize your product or service for you. This is the main value add of marketing in social networks—the social graph is available to you.

Justin Smith, Editor, InsideFacebook.com, the first blog devoted to Facebook and the Facebook Platform

Getting Started with Facebook

When you navigate your browser to Facebook at http://www.facebook.com, you see the page shown in Figure 1.1.

This page looks a little less than welcoming. To actually enter Facebook, sign up now. Enter your email address and a password in the boxes on the right, as well as your birthday. Click the Sign Up button to complete the sign-up process. Among that information is data that will appear on your profile—your geographic region and so on. (You'll see how to edit your profile later.)

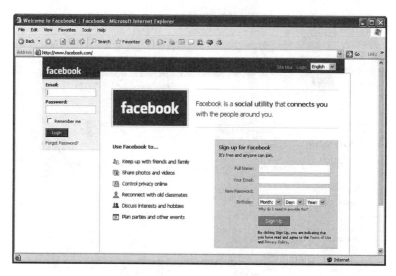

Figure 1.1
The Facebook start-up screen.

After your username (your email address) and password are set, you can enter them on the left in the www.facebook.com page, as shown in Figure 1.1. Click the "Remember me" check box to make Facebook automatically log you in every time you return.

After you've completed the sign-in process, you see the page shown in Figure 1.2, asking what you want to do next. This is your Facebook home page. It's always accessible by clicking the word Facebook in the upper left while you're logged in. (Note that the home page may have changed by the time you read this; Facebook is always tinkering with its appearance.)

Facebook offers the following items on the home page:

- Find Friends: Finding your friends makes your Facebook experience better. You can search for classmates or coworkers, for example.

- View your friends' profiles: Follow links to your friends' profiles to see what they've been doing on Facebook.

- View and edit your profile: Fill in details and upload a profile picture to help your friends recognize you.

Note that there's also a group of tabs near the top of the home page—Profile, Friends, and Inbox. Of these, the profile is where you typically spend the most time. It's how you present yourself publicly to other Facebook members.

Figure 1.2
The Facebook home page.

Here's an overview of these tabs. You'll spend a lot of time with them in Facebook:

- Profile: A user's profile is usually the center of his or her Facebook experience; it displays the user to the Facebook community. Your photo is here, your personal information (as much as you want to show), your mini-feed (which keeps you in touch with the activities of other friends), and so on. This is also where other users can drop in and leave you messages (on your "Wall," as you'll see shortly).

- Friends: The Friends tab opens the Friends page, where you manage and add friends. Here you can group your friends into lists, add or remove them, and more. This is a very important page for the friend-oriented Facebook user.

  In addition, this is where Facebook suggests people it thinks you might know, and whom you might want to become friends with.

- Inbox: This is the message center of Facebook. Here's where you read your messages. (By default, you're also notified at your regular email address when a Facebook user sends you a message—but you have to log into Facebook to read it.) Here you can compose, read, and send messages to other people, friends, and lists of friends.

  That's right—you can send messages to whole lists of friends (and each friend list can contain 1,500 friends). However, you have to be careful not to spam. Users can report you with a single click if you do spam, and you risk losing your account. We'll see how to create friend lists in this chapter.

Note that you can keep track of your friends' current status on the right side of Figure 1.2. For example, you can read that "Rodney Rumford is loving multiple social networks." You can set your status on your profile at any time, and any changes you make are updated on your friends' home pages.

Note also that at the bottom of the home page is your news feed. When you get some friends, you can keep track of their doings here. Take a look at the news feed shown in Figure 1.3.

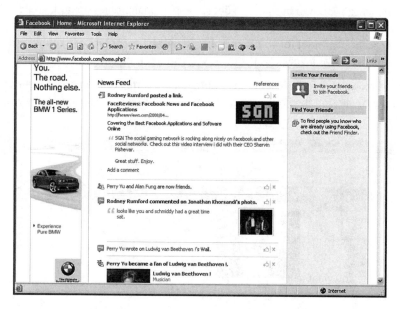

Figure 1.3
The home page's news feed.

Whenever a friend takes some public action (this person can decide what's publicly watchable), it shows up in the news feed. Later in this book, we'll look at how to use the news feed for business purposes.

The news feed is one of the most important parts of Facebook, because it keeps users in touch with what's going on with their friends, even when their friends don't know they're being watched. This feature is one of the primary reasons that people get obsessed with Facebook.

Because the Profile, Friends, and Inbox tabs are central to the Facebook experience, we'll look at each one in the following sections.

The Profile Tab

Your profile is your public face on Facebook. If you're a business, you might be loathe to put personal information on Facebook. Large corporations skip profiles and go directly to pages (see Chapter 3, "Creating Your Own Pages"). Pages are appropriate for businesses, bands, stars, and so on. Pages don't have friends; instead, they have fans.

But if you're not a large corporation yet, and you want to get some good Facebook publicity, I encourage you, as a business, to get some personal profiles going. If you don't want to do that, and you're not a known presence on the Internet yet, you might consider whether Facebook is right for you. Remember, it's all about content marketing, and you want to get people as involved with you as you can get them.

Figure 1.4 shows my profile (I admit the photo is a bit grim!). You can access your profile at any time by clicking the Profile tab that appears at the top of all pages while you're logged in.

Figure 1.4
My profile page, top half.

It's a long web page, so the bottom half appears in Figure 1.5.

Because the profile is so important, let's take it apart piece by piece.

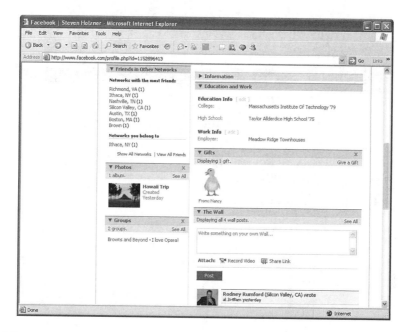

Figure 1.5
My profile page, bottom half.

Across the Top

Across the top of the profile page, you see the Facebook logo in the upper left. Clicking that at any time takes you back to your home page if you're logged in. You'll always see the Facebook logo and therefore can access your home page. You can also click the "home" link at the top right of any Facebook page to get back home. Also note the link next to the Profile tab that says "edit." You can edit your profile here, as you'll see in a moment.

The final elements across the top of the profile are these links:

- home: Takes you to your home page.
- account: Lets you set account info, such as credit card info in case you want to buy gifts.
- privacy: Lets you customize privacy settings, such as who can see what in your profile.
- logout: Logs you out.

The "account" link takes you to the page shown in Figure 1.6.

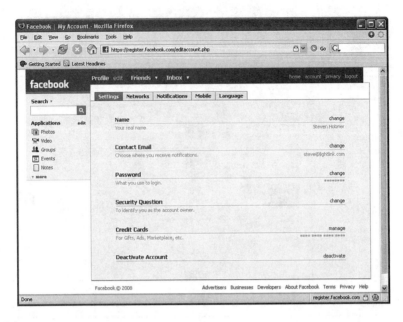

Figure 1.6
The account page.

On the account page, here are the items you can change:

- Name
- Contact Email
- Password
- Security Question: You can change the question Facebook asks you to verify that it's really you.
- Credit Cards: You can change or edit the credit card information you use to buy people gifts on Facebook.
- Deactivate Account

The "security" link takes you to the page shown in Figure 1.7.

Here are the items on the security page:

- Profile: Controls who can see what in your profile.
- Search: Controls how people can search for you.
- News Feed and Mini-Feed: Controls what's visible in the news feed and mini-feed.
- Applications: Controls the security settings for the Facebook applications you install.

We'll take another look at the security page soon. When you're on Facebook, security and privacy are major issues.

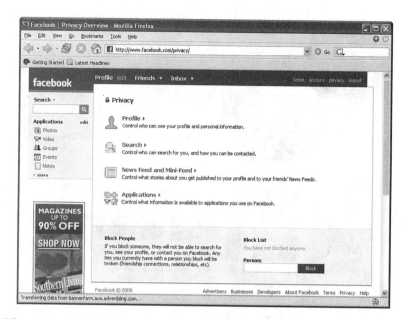

Figure 1.7
The security page.

The Search Bar

The search bar is directly under the Facebook logo in the upper left in Figure 1.4. You can search for people (as well as groups, events, applications, and so on) just by entering their name and pressing Enter.

Various search options are available. You can select them by clicking the down arrow next to the word Search. This opens the menu shown in the upper left of Figure 1.8.

The items on the search menu indicate the ways in which you can search:

- Basic Search
- Find Classmates
- Find Coworkers
- Profile Search
- Browse

Using this search box is a good way to reconnect with friends.

Figure 1.8
Search options.

Under the search box is a list of links; in my profile, they are as follows:

- Photos: Displays the photos you've uploaded—and photos from your friends.

- Video: Displays your videos—and videos from your friends.

- Groups: Displays the groups you belong to—and groups recently joined by your friends.

- Events: Lists the upcoming Facebook-registered events you may be connected to—and those of your friends.

- Notes: Allows you to publish commentary, which can include figures. Your friends can comment on your notes. And you can see your friends' notes as well.

Clicking any of these links takes you to a new page. For example, Figure 1.9 shows my notes page.

After I create this new note, a Notes section is added to my profile. It summarizes the new note so that friends visiting my profile can see there's a new note and read it. This offers marketing opportunities, because you can broadcast your notes to other friends. More about this is coming up later.

Finally, moving down in the search bar, underneath the Photos, Videos, Groups, and so on, is an ad. We'll have a great deal more to say about ads later in the book.

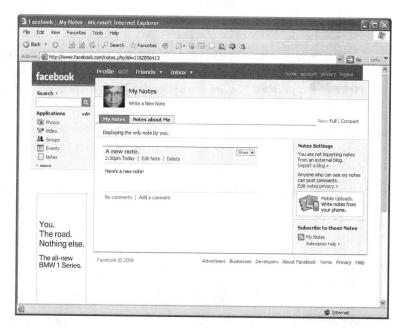

Figure 1.9
The notes page.

What, in your experience, is the single most important topic or technique to know about Facebook marketing?

Become a part of the online conversation and don't just throw up a display ad. Don't assume traditional targeting and banner creatives work within Facebook, because almost all users will simply tune out. Your audience on Facebook is primarily young adults that have been weaned on digital media who are very savvy when it comes to understanding whether they are being talked to or talked with in the online world. Talk with them by creating compelling content and applications that engage users so they share your messaging with their friends. The best advertising is a recommendation, and social networks' viral aspect enables advertisers to tap into this virality, assuming the message and the interaction with the consumer is right.

Eddie Smith, VP, Marketing & Business Development, SocialMedia Networks

Name, Photo, Networks, and Status

You can see my photo in my profile. If you want to upload or change your photo, just click the "edit" link on the Profile tab. Then click the Picture tab in the new window that opens, browse for a new photo with the Browse button, and upload the photo with the Upload Picture button.

Your name appears next to your photo, as shown in Figure 1.8. Want to change your name? Click the "account" link in the upper right of your profile, and then click the "change" link in the Name item.

Note also the status line that appears in my profile—"having fun," as shown in Figure 1.8. That status also appears in all your friends' home pages (as in "Steven is having fun"). You can set that status by clicking the status text ("is having fun"), entering your new text, and pressing Enter.

Setting your status can be a mild marketing opportunity. For example, if you were a shoe manufacturer, you might write "is enjoying his new spelunking shoes to the max." Unfortunately, you can't use any HTML, such as a link to your company's website.

You can, however, include an URL in your status. Facebook will treat it as a clickable URL.

Under your status are the networks you belong to, and your gender. As with nearly all items in your profile, these can be restricted, making them invisible to people you want to keep out.

Under my photo are five icons; they correspond to

- Education and Work
- Gifts
- Photos
- Groups
- The Wall

When you click an icon, the browser moves to the matching section in your profile. In other words, the same page stays open, but another section is moved to the top of the browser window. When you install Facebook applications on your profile, they each get an icon here too.

Note that above these icons are the words "I am online now.", indicating that I'm available for messages. If I weren't online, you'd see other items. In particular, you'd see links like these:

- View Photos of Steven (1)
- View Steven's Friends (6)
- Send Steven a Gift
- Send Steven a Message
- Poke Him!

Also note the link View My Friends (6) beneath my photo. If you click it, the browser navigates to the same page that clicking the Friends tab takes you to; this is discussed later in this chapter.

The Mini-Feed Section

On the right of Figure 1.8 is my mini-feed. This is the first of the profile "sections" we'll cover. A section in your profile has a title bar (reading "Mini-Feed" in this case), and you can rearrange sections in your profile just by dragging their title bars. So if you want the mini-feed to appear below the Photos section, just drag it there. Facebook will remember the new arrangement.

What's a mini-feed, and how does it differ from your news feed? As you saw on the home page, a news feed keeps you in contact with all your friends and what they're doing. You can also subscribe to various news sources in your news feed.

A mini-feed, on the other hand, appears on your profile page and includes items and updates about you. As you can see in Figure 1.8, for example, all the items in my mini-feed begin with my name, such as "Steven joined the group Browns and Beyond." We'll cover groups in detail in Chapter 2. A group lets friends connect around common interests, and they can leave messages for each other on the group's page.

In other words, my mini-feed keeps track of what I've been doing on Facebook for users who view my profile. (Again, you can set the access that various groups of users have to that information.) The items in the mini-feed are often hyperlinks. For example, "Browns and Beyond" in my mini-feed is a link to the group Browns and Beyond. In the mini-feed item "Steven added new photos to Hawaii Trip," Hawaii Trip is a link to my photo album of photos from our Hawaiian vacation. If you see someone's name (not your own) in your mini-feed, that's a link to that person's profile.

Note also the down-pointing arrow in the title bar of the mini-feed section. You can collapse or expand the sections in a profile by clicking that arrow. When you collapse a section, it closes to just its title bar, and the arrow turns into one that points to the right. (You can see an arrow like that in the Information section of my profile in Figure 1.5.)

The Friends and Friends in Other Networks Sections

You can see thumbnail photos of my friends in the Friends section of my profile in Figure 1.8. Clicking one of them takes you to that person's profile, which is pretty cool.

Directly under the Friends section in the profile is the Friends in Other Networks section, visible in Figure 1.5. There you can see a breakdown of my friends by network—Richmond, VA; Ithaca, NY; and so on. Clicking one of these networks opens a new page showing my friends in any of those networks. Figure 1.10 shows my friend in Ithaca, NY.

Figure 1.10

Friends in a network.

Note that there's also a "Networks you belong to" subsection at the bottom of the Friends in Other Networks section, as shown in Figure 1.5. As you can see, I belong to the Ithaca, NY network, which in my case is the default geographic network that Facebook always signs you up for.

You can join other networks if you like. Just click the "accounts" link in the upper right of any Facebook page after you're logged in. Click the Networks tab, opening the page shown in Figure 1.11.

You can join networks in this page. As the directions say, just enter a city, workplace, school, or region in the Network name box, and click Join Network.

Friends are the most intimate community you have in Facebook. After that, groups are the next community you can join—typically made up of groups of friends. After that come networks, which group people by city, workplace, school, or region. And you can set the privacy of your profile so that various pieces of data are restricted to friends and/or networks. It's all part of Facebook getting you involved.

Figure 1.11
Managing networks.

The Photos Section

The Photos section of your profile gives people access to any photos you've uploaded. These don't have to be personal photos. They can be business photos of products or catalog items.

In the Photos section of my profile are my Hawaii photos. Clicking that album opens it, as shown in Figure 1.12.

Want to create your own album? Click the Create a Photo Album link shown in Figure 1.12, which opens the page shown in Figure 1.13.

You can create a new photo album on this page, as I've done in Figure 1.13. This photo album is of my trip to Hawaii, but you can upload your business offerings, creating a rudimentary online catalog for interested friends.

You can also set who can see your new album, as shown in Figure 1.13, where I'm saying the Everyone can see the new album. Other choices limit viewership to your friends and your network, or friends of friends, or just friends.

Figure 1.12
Photo album overview.

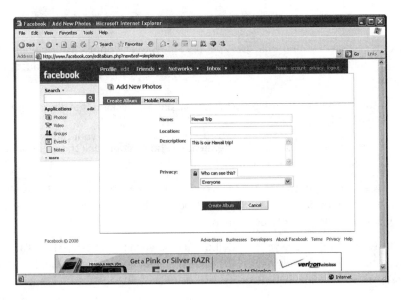

Figure 1.13
The Add New Photos page.

Clicking the Create Album button in Figure 1.13 takes you to a new page, as shown in Figure 1.14.

Figure 1.14

Adding photos to an album.

In Internet Explorer, Facebook asks you to install an ActiveX control to handle the upload-ing. Go ahead and install the ActiveX control (you have to click the yellow security bar that appears at the top of the display in Internet Explorer and select the Install item). When you install the ActiveX control, you see the display shown in Figure 1.14, where you can select the photos you want to upload to your new album.

When you click the Upload button in Figure 1.14, your photos are uploaded to Facebook.

How do you access the new album? You click the Photos icon in your profile and select the album you want, which opens the album. Nice.

The Groups Section

As you can see in Figure 1.5, under the Photos section is the Groups section, which lists the groups you belong to. I belong to two groups, and they're both listed.

As mentioned, groups are collections of users centered around a common interest, such as opera—which is why I belong to the I Love Opera! group. Clicking the I Love Opera! link in the Groups section of my profile opens the I Love Opera! group page, as shown in Figure 1.15.

Figure 1.15
The I Love Opera! group.

Groups are powerful tools for marketers, as discussed in Chapter 2.

The Information Section

Just under the mini-feed section is the Information section, as shown in the top right of Figure 1.5. This section displays the information you specified when creating your account, such as your email address and other contact info (again, you can restrict who gets to see this information).

You can fill out your profile, adding more information than the basics Facebook asks for when you sign up. We'll cover how to edit your profile in a few pages.

Be careful what you make publicly visible in your Information section. There might be no need for casual browsers to see your email address, for example. You can set privacy levels using the "privacy" link that appears on any Facebook page when you're logged in. We'll cover that in this chapter as well.

The Education and Work Section

As you can also see on the right of Figure 1.5, your profile also contains an Education and Work section, allowing you to list your high school and college, as well as your place of work. In fact, Facebook asks you for this information when you sign up.

Like the Information section, you can restrict who gets to see what information in your Education and Work section.

The Gifts Section

You can give gifts to others in Facebook; they appear in the Gifts section of your profile. As you can see in Figure 1.5, someone sent me a duck, one of the few free gifts on Facebook.

Usually, gifts aren't free—you have to pay for them. It doesn't mean anything more than just getting a virtual gift that you can display, but it costs real money. The fact that thousands of people buy gifts is a testament to the power of Facebook as a marketing tool.

The Wall Section

At the bottom right of Figure 1.5, you can see the Wall section—a wildly popular item in Facebook. Here you can leave messages, links, or videos for others.

The Wall is a way to connect to your friends. As you see in Figure 1.5, some of my friends have been connecting to me. You can even leave yourself a note on the Wall. Just type into the "Write something on your own Wall..." box and click the Post button. You can attach video and links with the links under that box.

When you get a message on your Wall, several links appear at the bottom of the new message. For example, if you get a message from Albert Einstein, you see a link to "Write on Albert's Wall," which allows you to get back to Einstein immediately by writing on his Wall.

There's also a Message link, that, when clicked, opens the Message system. You can message the person who posted on your Wall. All you have to do is to enter your subject and your message and click Send.

There's also a Delete link that lets you delete Wall posts, which is a good idea when things start to get too cluttered.

That completes our overview of what's in your Facebook profile. Your profile might acquire more sections over time. For example, as you add Facebook applications (discussed in Chapters 9 and 10), each application may get a new, titled section in your profile.

What if you want to change your profile information? That's easy.

Editing Your Profile

You can edit your profile at any time. Just click the "edit" link on the Profile tab. This opens the profile editor, shown in Figure 1.16.

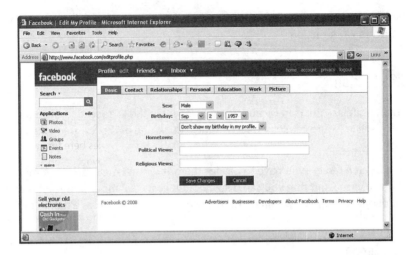

Figure 1.16
Editing your profile.

Facebook wants you to enter as much information about yourself as it can get. Although you might think that's not a good idea, there are trade-offs—ones that might be of interest to marketers. The more information you enter, the more Facebook targets the unsolicited information it sends you.

In other words, Facebook targets ads to specific demographics in a way that's more precise than just about any other marketing platform you can name. That's one reason your marketing dollars on Facebook can go further than many other places.

Another aspect of the unsolicited information that Facebook hones according to the information you give it about yourself has to do with which friends it suggests you might want to add. And that can be useful.

Facebook is always after you to add more information to your profile. For example, if you open the Information section in your profile, you'll probably see a yellow box with a link to "Fill out your Profile." That link opens the profile editor shown in Figure 1.16.

The tabs in the Facebook profile editor are as follows:

- Basic: This is basic information, such as sex, birthday, hometown, and so on, but the information here can get pretty personal—such as what your religious beliefs are.

- Contact: This tab asks for your contact information. It's pretty probing, asking for your phone number, cell number, email address, and street address.

  You might feel queasy about supplying such a depth of personal information, and if so, by all means, don't. Many young people, raised in an environment where everything is shared, seem to have no problems putting down the most intimate details. But that doesn't mean you have to.

If you're a marketer, on the other hand, this may be information that you'd love to share—such as your phone number. Note that there's also space for a website URL here—prime contact info for businesses.

- Relationships: This is where you can use Facebook as a dating service. You can list yourself as single or "In an open relationship." And you can indicate your specific relationship preference by selecting a check box in the "Interested in:" section: Men or Women. The "Looking for:" section lets you check Friendship, Dating, A Relationship, or Networking.

- Personal: This tab lets you list your interests. There are text boxes here for Activities, Interests, Favorite Music, Favorite TV Shows, Favorite Movies, Favorite Books, Favorite Quotes, and About Me.

- Education: The Education tab lets you list—surprise!—your education history. You can list your high school and multiple colleges/universities, including your major.

- Work: There are boxes on this tab for Employer, Position, Description, City/Town, and Time Period. There's no option if you're an employer or self-employed, though.

- Picture: This tab allows you to upload the profile photo you want and delete photos you don't like.

You won't edit your profile every day, but it's good to know that you can do so when needed.

But what about that sensitive data you entered? How can you restrict who sees it? For that, take a look at the next topic.

Setting Profile Privacy

As mentioned, privacy is a big issue on Facebook. Fortunately, you can set the privacy level for a great number of items in Facebook.

To customize your privacy settings, click the "privacy" link in the upper left of any Facebook page when you're logged in. You see the page shown in Figure 1.17.

The sections shown in Figure 1.17 are as follows:

- Profile: Controls who can see your profile and personal information.

- Search: Controls who can search for you and how you can be contacted.

- News Feed and Mini-Feed: Controls what stories about you get published to your profile and to your friends' news feeds.

- Applications: Controls what information is available to applications you use on Facebook.

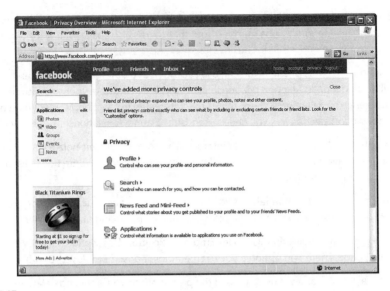

Figure 1.17
Setting your privacy.

Let's look at the profile security settings. Click the Profile link, opening the page shown in Figure 1.18.

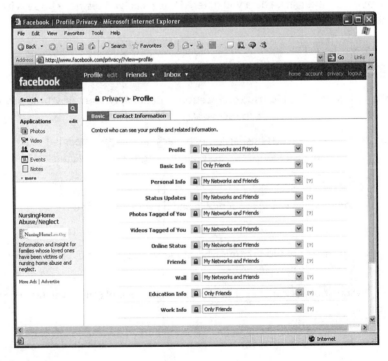

Figure 1.18
Setting your profile privacy.

Note that the Basic tab is chosen by default. Here are the items in this tab:

- Profile: Controls who can see your profile.

- Basic Info: Sets access to your Sex, Birthday, Hometown, Political Views, and Religious Views.

- Personal Info: Sets access to your Activities, Interests, Favorite Music, Favorite TV Shows, Favorite Movies, Favorite Books, Favorite Quotes, and About Me.

- Status Updates: Sets access to your status data (such as "Steven Holzner is having fun.").

- Photos Tagged of You: When you upload photos, you can tag each one with the names of the people in the photo. This box lets you set access to such photos.

- Videos Tagged of You: You can also tag uploaded videos with people's names. This box lets you set access to such videos.

- Online Status: Specifies whether people can see if you're online.

- Friends: Controls access to your friends list.

- Wall: Controls access to your Wall.

- Education Info: Controls access to your education info—college and the like.

- Work Info: Controls access to your job info.

Each of these items can be set—using the drop-down list box next to it—to one of these values:

- My Networks and Friends

- Friends of Friends

- Only Friends

- Customize

As you can see, the primary groups you can restrict access to are the groups that social life on Facebook revolves around—friends and networks. Friends you select yourself, but by choosing a network, you may be letting in swarms of people you don't know, so being able to restrict network access is great.

In fact, you might want to restrict the access of certain networks while allowing access by others. That's what the Customize item is for. Clicking that item displays the window shown in Figure 1.19.

Using the customize window, you can admit everyone in the Ithaca, NY network while excluding everyone in the Gonzo Wackos network. (Actually, there is no such network—not yet, anyway.)

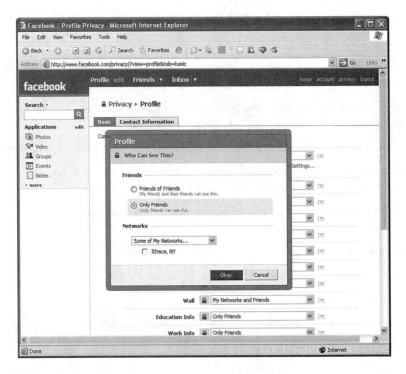

Figure 1.19
Customizing network privacy.

That's all fine, but what about the more personal information, such as your email address, home address, and phone numbers? You don't have to share your address or phone numbers with Facebook, but you need to give Facebook your email address, or it won't open an account for you.

You set the privacy of these items using the Contact Information tab, as shown in Figure 1.20.

Here are the contact information items you can set privacy for:

- IM Screen Name
- Mobile Phone
- Land Phone
- Current Address
- Website
- Email

As with the Basic privacy information, you can set these items to My Networks and Friends, Friends of Friends, Only Friends, or Customize.

Figure 1.20
Setting your contact information privacy.

That completes our overview of setting profile privacy items. As you can see, you can restrict access to your data. But note that the most restrictive settings still allow friends, so if you're a privacy freak, plan accordingly.

That completes the first of the three main tabs you see in every Facebook window when you're logged in—the Profile tab (including the edit link in that tab). There are two more tabs—Friends and Inbox—and we'll take a look at them next.

The Friends Tab

The Friends tab is all about managing your friends. How do you acquire friends on Facebook?

Searching for Friends

You do a search. Just enter the name of someone you're searching for in the Search box in the upper left, and press Enter. A list of matches to your search appears, as shown in Figure 1.21.

Figure 1.21
Searching for potential friends.

Note the Add to Friends link next to the first match. Clicking that link opens the page shown in Figure 1.22, which allows you to add a personal greeting to your prospective friend.

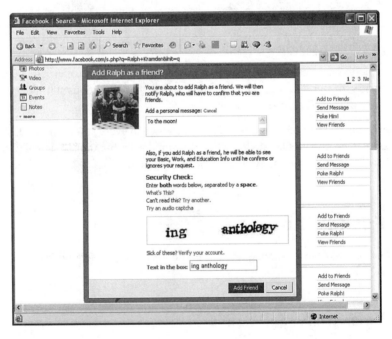

Figure 1.22
Adding a friend.

Facebook also displays a graphic with two words in it that you're supposed to enter, as shown in Figure 1.22. You'll see this every time you want to send a message; it's a spam-avoidance measure. (If you're thinking of spamming Facebook messages on behalf of a business, you should rethink.) Clicking the Add Friend button sends this message to your prospective friend by email, and a link if he agrees to add you as a friend. After this person adds you, he appears in your collection of friends.

Managing Your Friends

To manage your friends, click the Friends tab, opening the page shown in Figure 1.23.

Figure 1.23
Managing your friends.

Want to leave a message on somebody's Wall? Just click her image, and you'll go to her profile.

By default, all your friends are displayed, but you can look at various subsets. Clicking the down arrow on the Friends tab displays the menu shown in Figure 1.24.

Figure 1.24
The Friends tab's menu.

The items are as follows:

- Status Updates: Shows friends with updated status lines.

- Online Now: Shows your friends who are online now.

- Recently Updated: Shows which of your friends have recently updated their profiles.

- Recently Added: Shows your most recently added friends.

- All Friends: Shows all your friends (the default).

- Invite Friends: Allows you to email friends who aren't already on Facebook to invite them to join.

- Find Friends: Opens a page that has various ways of searching for prospective friends.

For example, selecting the Online Now item opens the page shown in Figure 1.25, listing which of my friends are online right now.

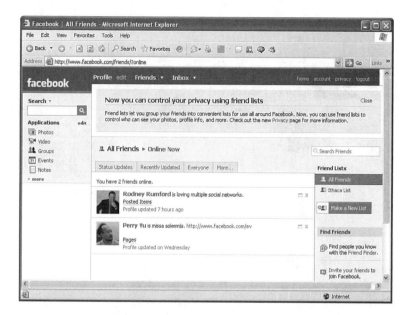

Figure 1.25
Which of my friends are online now.

Creating Friend Lists

You can also organize your friends into lists, which is convenient when you want to email a bunch of friends at once. You can have up to 1,500 friends in a list, which is good for getting the word out.

To create a friends list, click the Make a New List button on the right of the Friends tab. Enter the name of the new list, as shown in Figure 1.26 (in this case, that's Ithaca List).

The next step is to add the friends you want in the new list, as shown in Figure 1.27. Here you type the names of the friends you want to add—or you can select multiple friends at once using the Select Multiple Friends link.

Figure 1.26
Creating a new friend list.

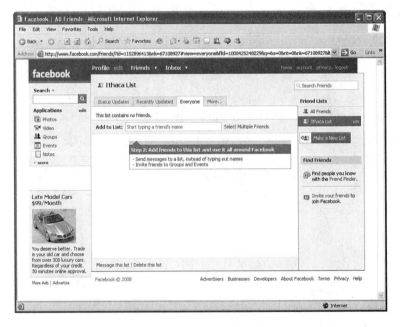

Figure 1.27
Selecting friends.

As you add new friends to the list, they appear on the page, as shown in Figure 1.28.

Figure 1.28
Adding friends.

Later you can manage the list using the "Manage this list" and "Delete this list" links you see near the bottom of Figure 1.28.

That introduces as much as you need to know about friends and managing friends for the chapters to come.

Next up: the Inbox tab.

The Inbox Tab

Clicking the Inbox tab displays the page shown in Figure 1.29.

As you can gather from the name, the Inbox is how you handle messages in Facebook. The name is actually somewhat of a misnomer, because you send messages from here as well (although Inandoutbox doesn't have quite the same ring to it).

Five tabs are visible in Figure 1.29:

- Inbox: Shows your inbound messages.

- Sent Messages: Shows your sent messages.

- Notifications: Shows your notifications, which happen when someone adds you as a friend or writes on your Wall.

- Updates: Shows the updates Facebook wants you to know about.

- Compose Message: Lets you create messages and send them.

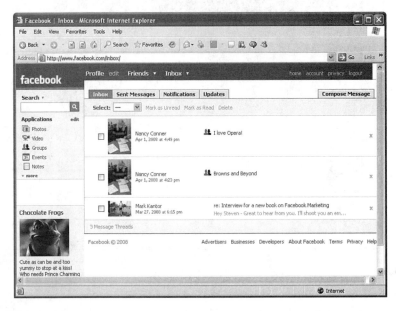

Figure 1.29
The Inbox.

Reading Messages

Want to read an entire message based on the summary you see in the Inbox? Just click the text of the message in the overview. A new page with the full message appears, as shown in Figure 1.30.

You can type a reply and click Send to answer the sender.

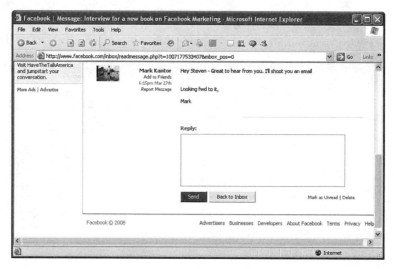

Figure 1.30
Examining a message in the Inbox.

Avoiding Spam

If you receive a message from someone who isn't your friend, you see the Report Message link when you read the message, as shown in Figure 1.30. You can use it to report a message as spam. Here's what Facebook's help topic on Report Message says:

"I was warned for sending spam messages.

"You received this warning because you sent messages that other users reported as spam. Facebook does not allow users to send messages promoting or advertising a product, service, or opportunity. In order to prevent this from happening in the future, please refrain from sending messages of this kind."

Obviously, you want to avoid spamming members using messages, or you could lose your Facebook account.

Reading Notifications

Also check out the Notifications tab, shown in Figure 1.31.

Your news feed tells you what your friends are doing, your mini-feed tells your friends what you are doing, and your notifications tell you what's been happening to you.

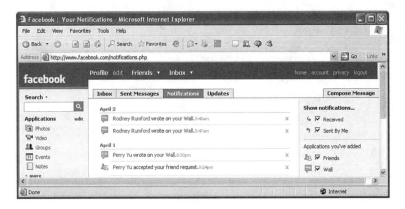

Figure 1.31
Some notifications.

Composing Messages

You can create and send messages by clicking the Compose Message tab, as shown in Figure 1.32.

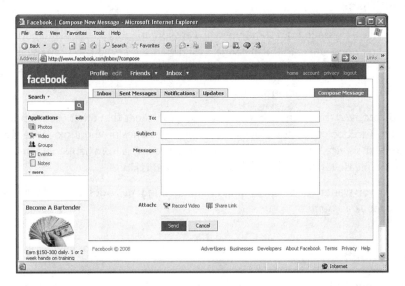

Figure 1.32
Composing a message.

Type the name of a friend, a friend list, or an email address in the To: box. Enter the subject of the message in the Subject box and the body of the message in the Message box. Attach any videos or links you want, and click Send. Presto.

We're almost done with this foundation chapter. But what would an introduction to an online resource be without the help system?

Getting Help

You can access Facebook's help files by clicking the Help link at the bottom right of any page. Clicking the link opens the page shown in Figure 1.33.

Figure 1.33
The help page.

Note in particular the Getting Started Guide link at the top of the help page. That link used to be the first thing you saw on your home page—until recently, when Facebook moved it to the help page.

The Getting Started Guide, shown in Figure 1.34, is a fine resource for new Facebook users.

In the guide, you'll find information on—most important in Facebook—how to find friends, how to search for coworkers and classmates, and how to search by name. You'll also find a tour of what Facebook has to offer; it's extremely useful to new Facebook users.

In other words, the Getting Started Guide is highly recommended.

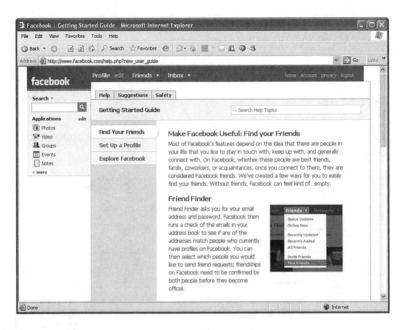

Figure 1.34
The Getting Started Guide.

The rest of the help system is set up as a FAQ (Frequently Asked Questions) list. For example, selecting the Friends and Networks link in Figure 1.33 takes you to the friends FAQ.

Questions in the friends FAQ function as links to explanatory articles:

How do I add a friend?

How do I suggest a friend to someone?

Is there a way to cancel a friend request?

If I ignore a friend request, will they find out?

How do I remove a friend?

If I remove someone as a friend, will they be notified?

Who shows up in the "friends box" on my profile?

FAQs are fine, but if you're like me, you want to be able to contact someone in case your question isn't in the FAQs (although, they are pretty thorough). You can contact a real person for help at http://www.facebook.com/help/contact_generic.php, as shown in Figure 1.35.

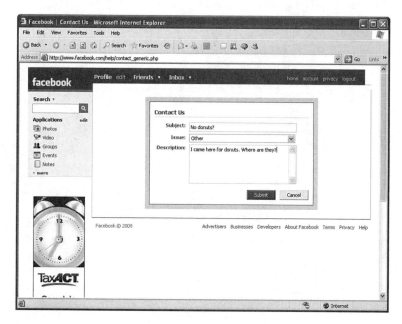

Figure 1.35
Contacting a real person for help.

Facebook Groups

In this chapter:

Welcome to groups

Joining groups

Creating groups

Using groups from a marketing perspective

Commercializing your group

Customizing your group

Welcome to Facebook Groups

Groups are the oldest way to aggregate users on Facebook and are an appropriate starting point for our marketing discussion. If your group is something special, it'll take off on Facebook. Groups have been known to start from nothing and have more than one million members at the end of a week. Groups are Facebook pages where members can interact with each other and start discussions. Creating your own group can get quite a buzz about your brand.

But as with all Facebook marketing, remember the primary rule: content marketing (that is, you have to provide interesting content, not just an ad message). Facebook members will follow your lead, and your marketing efforts will go viral if they're interesting to people on Facebook. It's not a place where you can overwhelm people with big advertising budgets.

A group gives you a central place to create a community and generate interest in your brand. You can draw customers, friends, and curious onlookers to groups. Bear in mind that what will happen, however, is a discussion—a two-way conversation. If you're not prepared for that, you might think about another marketing option (such as pages, discussed in the next chapter). Besides text, you can also post photos and video to groups, good opportunities for marketers.

Messaging Your Members

You can send messages to the members of your group en masse. You must avoid the appearance of spamming, however, because Facebook users can still report your messages (which arrive in users' Inboxes).

If your group gets too popular—more than 1,200 members is the usual limit that Facebook mentions—Facebook will not let you send messages en masse anymore, so that's something to keep in mind. Although Facebook has said that it will remove this restriction, it's still there.

People can invite other friends to join a group, so if there is interest in your group, it can grow quickly through the Facebook equivalent of word of mouth. In addition, the groups people belong to appear on people's profile pages—which can be a bumper sticker for your group.

A Word About Spam

Note also that if your group becomes large, spammers will inevitably show up, and you must be vigilant about removing the spam. Spam and spammers are easy to remove on Facebook, but they always crop up again. If your group is getting big and you want to retain the ability to mass-message, think about a page instead—pages are like profiles for public and corporate entities. (Another advantage of pages over groups is that you can host Facebook applications in pages, but not in groups—and that can be powerful for marketers.)

Spammers typically work by posting links to their own groups or websites on existing groups. Facebook frowns on this. Although spammers can get away with this on a limited scale, Facebook's robots watch all groups at all times, and big-time spammers' accounts are invariably shut down in short order.

So, the word is, don't spam.

About the best alternative is to use social ads to boost your group, or to start talking to other group administrators about link exchanges. You used to be able to create sponsored groups.

Here's how Facebook describes sponsored groups (note the defensive tone):

"These groups are paid promotions by outside companies. The sponsor controls the look and feel of the group, but does not have access to personal information or profiles. The money from these promotions, like the money from all our ads, goes towards the Facebook's server and operational costs. Sponsored groups help us keep the service free and fast."

So are sponsored groups a good deal? Nope—they don't even exist anymore. They've been replaced by pages, discussed in the next chapter.

Things are changing rapidly for marketers on Facebook. In fact, Facebook now offers dedicated teams to implement all your advertising, including planning your campaign—if you have an advertising budget that exceeds $50,000 a year. In this book, I'm assuming you don't have that kind of money for advertising, which means that Facebook expects you to do everything yourself, using its online interfaces. And that's what this book is about.

While we're on the subject of groups, here's the word from Facebook on offensive groups:

"Groups that attack a specific person or group of people (e.g. racist, sexist, or other hate groups) will not be tolerated. Creating such a group will result in immediate termination of your Facebook account."

That's an overview of groups from a marketing perspective. Now let's cover the details of joining and creating groups on Facebook.

Joining Facebook Groups

Getting familiar with Facebook groups is easy—you just need to find the groups you're interested in and join them. We'll take a look at the process now, and then get a guided tour of how to create your own group(s).

What Groups Are Available?

How do you find which groups are available on Facebook? Say you want to find groups for beach lovers. How do you do that?

Clicking the Groups icon at the left on your profile page opens your groups management page, as shown in Figure 2.1.

This page has two primary sections—a list of the groups your friends have joined, and a list of your groups that have recently been updated. Facebook, as the ultimate social network, lists groups that your friends are joining to get you involved.

If you want to see what a group is all about, just click its image or name on this page, and you go to the group's page.

Note also the My Groups tab in Figure 2.1. Clicking it opens a window that shows you the groups you belong to, as shown in Figure 2.2.

Figure 2.1
A Facebook groups management page.

Figure 2.2
The I Love Opera! group.

Note that each group has a name, profile photo, and information about its size and type.

Note that Facebook lists the group's news in summary fashion: 33 More Members, 2 Board Topics, and 2 Wall Posts. Board topics are how members talk with each other. (What does "Network: Global" mean? More on that in a few pages.)

How do you search for groups you might be interested in? There are three ways—search for them, browse for them, and check out the popular groups list. (These methods are in addition to the groups that Facebook displays your friends as having joined.)

To search for groups you might be interested in, go back to your groups management page (click the Groups icon on the left of any Facebook page while you're logged in), enter a keyword or keywords in the Search for Groups box, and press Enter.

For example, say that you're looking for groups about beaches. Figure 2.3 shows the results when you search for "beach."

Figure 2.3
Searching for beach groups.

If you see a group you like, click it to open the group's page.

You can also browse for groups. Just click the Browse Groups tab on your groups management page.

In addition, you can browse the most popular groups by clicking the Popular Groups tab on your groups management page. Doing so opens the page shown in Figure 2.4.

Figure 2.4
Looking at the most popular groups.

Figure 2.5 shows the networks activity page, which you'll see more of in Chapter 6, "Optimizing and Monitoring Your Advertising." It's opened to the Groups tab. Facebook is showing you the most popular groups for your network. There's also a Popular Today list of global (not tied to a specific network) groups on the right of this page.

Figure 2.5
The network activity page.

Suppose you see a group you like. What's actually in a group?

What insightful pieces of advice would you most want new marketers on Facebook to know?

Facebook users like playing, sharing, and interacting with friends within Facebook's walled garden. This environment provides users with a relatively uncluttered, familiar place to socialize with friends. Users become uncomfortable when you redirect them out of this environment and annoyed if you make their familiar pages cluttered or present them with ad creative that distracts from the social experience. Figure out how to get users to interact with your ads and keep them within Facebook by redirecting them to an application running in the Facebook environment. This keeps the user comfortable, makes it easy for the user to share the application (and your messaging) with friends, and provides them with an easy way to reaccess and use your application. Stay away from the classic "click on your ad and redirect to my website approach," as you'll not tap into what social networks are all about with this approach.

Eddie Smith, VP, Marketing & Business Development, SocialMedia Networks

Taking a Look at a Group

Say that you've identified a new group that you want to look at, such as No Tenors Allowed, an opera group. How do you see what's going on with that group? You look at the group's page by clicking its photo or name in your search results.

Figures 2.6 and 2.7 are the top half and bottom half of the No Tenors Allowed group.

This is the group's main page and focal point. This is where the action is.

The following sections are on the left of the page:

- Recent News: News posted by the group's administrators
- Photos: Photos uploaded by members
- Videos: Videos uploaded by members
- Posted Items: Special items that have been posted to the group
- Discussion Board: Interactive posts by members
- Members: Lists the people who belong to the group
- The Wall: Like your personal Wall, but for the group

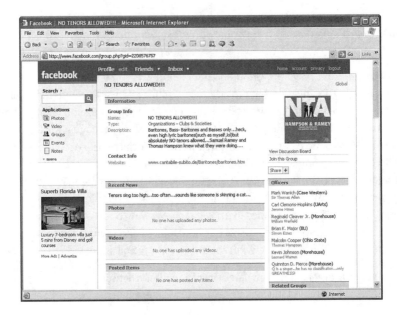

Figure 2.6
The No Tenors Allowed group, top half.

Figure 2.7
The No Tenors Allowed group, bottom half.

The following sections are on the right:

- Officers: The people who govern the group
- Related Groups: A list of like groups for you to browse
- Group Type: The type of group. Here you can find out, for example, if the group is open to new members.
- Admins: The administrator(s) responsible for the group's day-to-day activities

The discussion board is the heart of a group. It's made up of back-and-forth chatter from members of the group. Until you join a group, you can't participate fully in the discussion board (such as posting new topics). Let's look at a discussion board for a group I belong to—I Love Opera!, shown in Figure 2.8.

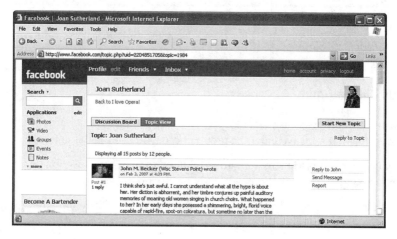

Figure 2.8
A discussion board.

The discussion board is one of the most important things that makes a group a group, because it's where members of the group can post back and forth. If you are marketing something, this is where Facebook users will discuss it.

So that, in summary, is how groups look and work on Facebook. Groups provide central meeting places for Facebook members with common interests. If you look at a group's page that you belong to, as shown in Figure 2.9, you'll see an Invite People to Join link at the bottom right.

This link is a very important one for marketers, because it allows groups to grow in a viral fashion. If your group is of interest to Facebook users, you'll know it.

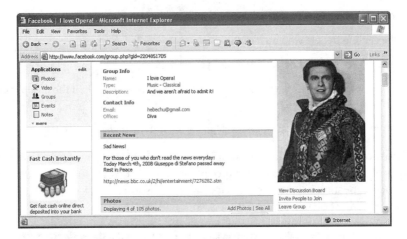

Figure 2.9
The Invite People to Join link.

How Do I Join a Group?

Joining an open group is easy. Just navigate to an open group's page, and click the Join this Group link that appears under the group photo (you can see this link in Figure 2.6).

When you join a group, a link to that group is added to the Groups section on your profile page, making reaching that group as easy as clicking the link.

However, determining exactly which groups you can join is a different matter, as discussed next.

Which Groups Can I Join?

On Facebook, you can join up to 200 groups. Two primary types of groups are open to you—*global* and *network* groups. Anyone can join an open global group. You can also join any open group that's in your network.

What's this "open" stuff? Aren't all Facebook groups open?

No, they aren't. In fact, there are three types of groups; here's how Facebook describes them:

- "Open: For 'global' groups, everyone on Facebook can view the group and join. If the group is exclusive to a specific network, only the people on that network can become a member. The Wall, discussion board, and photos are all visible to anyone viewing the group.

- "Closed: For 'global' groups, everyone on Facebook can see the group, but the administrators must approve all membership requests or personally send invites. If the group is exclusive to one network, only people on that network can see the group. Only group members can view the Wall, discussion board, and photos. If you are not a member, you will not receive News Feed stories about closed groups.

- "Secret: These groups cannot be found in searches or viewed by non-members. The name of the group will not display on the profiles of members. Membership is by invitation only. Non-members will not receive News Feed stories about secret groups."

If you're a group administrator, you can change these options for your group at any time by clicking Edit Group Profile.

Note also that you can invite any of your Facebook friends to join a global group. However, if the group is network-specific, you can invite only friends who are members of your network.

You can also invite people who are not yet Facebook members to join a group, but they have to join Facebook first. To invite them, give their email address after clicking the "Invite People to Join" link.

You can upload photos to a group you've joined if the group's administrator has allowed photos to be posted, as set on the group's Edit Group Profile page. (Note that even if the admin has allowed photos to be uploaded, he or she still can specify if everyone can upload photos or only other admins.)

If allowed, click Add Photos on the group's page. You can upload up to five photos at once, or as many as you want from an existing Facebook album.

Photos on secret and closed groups can be viewed only by members of the group. Admins can remove any photos they want.

You can also upload videos if the group's administrator(s) have allowed videos on the Edit Group Profile page. As with photos, even if they allow videos, admins can restrict video uploading either to all members or to other admins.

If you can post videos, click Add Videos on the groups main page. You have three options: Add from My Videos, Upload File, and Record Video. Note that videos on secret and closed groups can be viewed only by members of the group. As with photos, note that admins can remove any videos they want.

This gives us a good foundation for groups. As a marketer, you probably want to create your own group(s)—and we'll look at how that works now.

Creating Your Own Facebook Groups

To create your own group, click your Groups link on the left of any logged-in Facebook page. Doing so opens the Groups management page, as shown in Figure 2.10.

Figure 2.10
The Groups management page.

Click the Create a New Group button on the right to open the page shown in Figure 2.11.

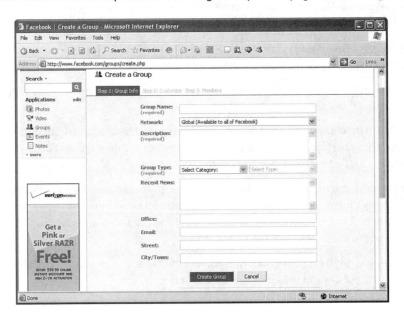

Figure 2.11
The Create a Group page.

Let's create your new group.

Creating Your Group

In this case, we'll create a fictitious company, Beach Bum Rentals, that will rent beach space on Waikiki beach to beach bums. This is nice work if you can get it, because space on Waikiki beach is free.

Here are the items you need to fill in:

- Group Name: This required field gives the name of your new group. We'll use Beach Bum Rentals here.

- Network: You can choose from any of the networks you belong to, or Global, which means that the new group will be available to all Facebook members. Hoping to attract business, we'll make our group global.

- Description: Here's where you can describe the group. Prospective group members can read this required information, so make sure it's alluring. We'll make our description "Want space on Waikiki beach? We'll rent it to you! 3 x 6 sections available, as well as the premiere 4 x 8. Reasonable monthly rates."

- Group Type: This required field is where you specify the type of your group. We'll select Business here, because Beach Bum Rentals is a business. The possible choices are

  - Business
  - Common Interest
  - Entertainment & Arts
  - Geography
  - Internet & Technology
  - Just for Fun
  - Music
  - Organizations
  - Sports & Recreation
  - Student Groups

  You must also select a subtype for your group. Because we're all about renting beach space, we'll choose Real Estate.

- Recent News: As you've seen, admins can post recent news items on their group page. "Our premiere sections are going fast! At only $3,000 a month, prices may never be this low again!"

- Office: Here's where you can list your office.

- Email: You can also list an email for the group.

- Street: The street address of your business.

- City/Town: The city/town of your business.

Figure 2.12 shows the filled-in information form.

Click the Create Group button to create your new group.

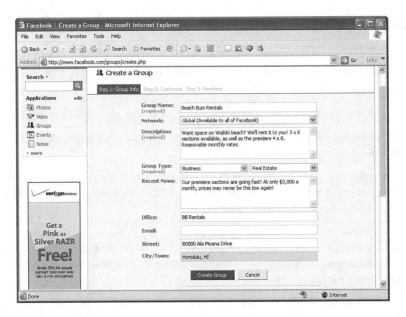

Figure 2.12
Filling in information for a new group.

Customizing Your Group

The next step is to customize your new group, as shown in Figures 2.13 and 2.14.

First you upload a photo for your new group. We'll use a photo of Waikiki beach, as shown in Figure 2.13.

Next, you fill in information about your new group:

- Website: The group's website, if any.
- Options:
  - Show related groups: Check this item if you want Facebook to show related groups on your group's page.
  - Enable discussion board: Check this item to turn on the discussion board. You don't need to do this. It's always somewhat of a risk to have Facebook users discuss what you have to offer, but your group won't become popular (unless you're already well-known) without a discussion board.
  - Enable the Wall: You don't have to enable the Wall, but without it, you might as well have a page, not a group. The Wall is part of the interactivity that Facebook users expect from a group, so it's a good idea to turn it on and accept user comments.

Figure 2.13
Customizing your new group, top half.

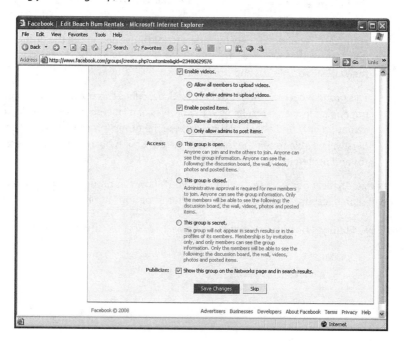

Figure 2.14
Customizing your new group, bottom half.

- Enable photos: By default, members can upload photos. You might want to turn this one off.

  - Allow all members to upload photos

  - Only allow admins to upload photos

- Enable videos: By default, members can upload videos. You might also want to turn this one off.

  - Allow all members to upload videos.

  - Only allow admins to upload videos.

- Enable posted items: Posted items work like a bulletin board. For maximum communication with your members, leave the "Allow all members to post items." item selected. A more common selection for businesses is "Only allow admins to post items."

  - Allow all members to post items.

  - Only allow admins to post items.

- Access: Here you specify whether your group is open, closed (but still visible), or secret:

  - This group is open: Here's how Facebook describes this option: "Anyone can join and invite others to join. Anyone can see the group information. Anyone can see the following: the discussion board, the Wall, videos, photos and posted items."

  - This group is closed: Here's how Facebook describes this option: "Administrative approval is required for new members to join. Anyone can see the group information. Only the members will be able to see the following: the discussion board, the Wall, videos, photos and posted items."

  - This group is secret: Here's how Facebook describes this option: "The group will not appear in search results or in the profiles of its members. Membership is by invitation only, and only members can see the group information. Only the members will be able to see the following: the discussion board, the Wall, videos, photos and posted items."

- Publicize: As Facebook says, this option lets you "Show this group on the Networks page and in search results." Businesses usually want this option left on.

Click the Save Changes button, as shown in Figure 2.14. You see the page shown in Figure 2.15.

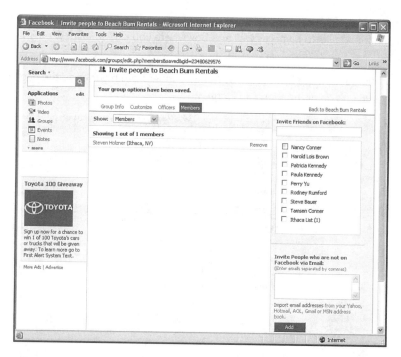

Figure 2.15
Group options have been saved.

What, in your experience, is the single most important topic or technique to know about Facebook marketing? What do Facebook users want?

Facebook users do not like spam, and personally most Internet users hate spam as well. A lot of Facebook advertisers start to bombard their group members or fans with messages and annoying advertisements. Instead of driving traffic to your product this turns off the average person. If your product is good, it creates its own demand over the social networks and if it's really good, it spreads like fire, better than any advertising technique a company might spend thousands of dollars on.

Sunmit Singh, CEO, RootsGear, Inc., www.rootsgear.com

Inviting Friends to Join Your Group

As shown in Figure 2.15, you can invite friends to join your new group—including inviting whole friend lists at the same time.

This page lists you as a member of the new group. On the right, you see a list of your friends and friend lists to invite, as well as a box where you can email new prospective members.

When you click a friend to invite, such as Nancy Conner from my friends, the page displays that person's name, as shown in Figure 2.16.

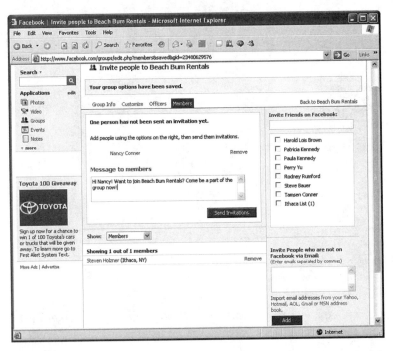

Figure 2.16
Inviting new friends.

As shown in the figure, we're about to send Nancy an enticing invitation: "Hi Nancy! Want to join Beach Bum Rentals? Come be a part of the group now!"

When you click the Send Invitations button, you see a page indicating that your message has been sent, as shown in Figure 2.17.

Here's the message that Nancy receives:

Steven invited you to join the Facebook group "Beach Bum Rentals".

Steven says, "Hi Nancy! Want to join Beach Bum Rentals? Come be a part of the group now!"

To see more details and confirm this group invitation, follow the link below: [URL]

Thanks,

The Facebook Team

Figure 2.17
Inviting a new friend.

Note the links near the top of this new page in Figure 2.17. They let you edit what you've just entered about your new group:

- Group Info

- Customize

- Officers

- Members

Click the Officers link now. You see the page shown in Figure 2.18.

I'll make myself an officer of the group by clicking the make officer link next to my name. Facebook asks for your position, as shown in Figure 2.19. I'll add myself as CEO.

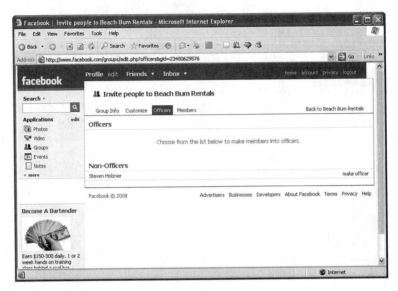

Figure 2.18
Creating a new officer.

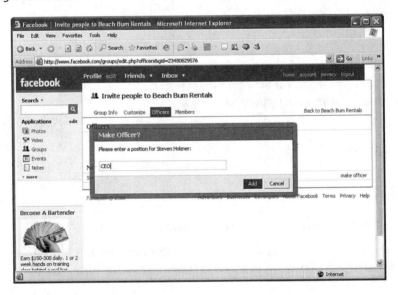

Figure 2.19
Making myself the CEO.

You can see me as the new CEO in the page that appears, as shown in Figure 2.20.

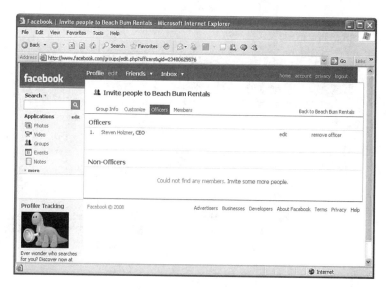

Figure 2.20
I'm the new CEO.

Seeing Your New Group

To see your new group, click the Back to Beach Bum Rentals link in the upper right of Figure 2.20. This opens your new group, as shown in Figure 2.21.

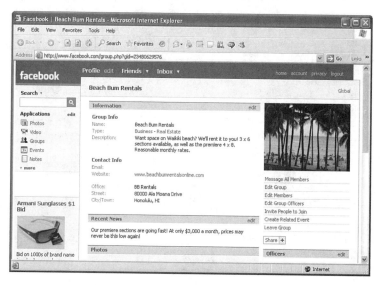

Figure 2.21
Your new group.

Voila! Your new group is in business.

Now any members can post to your discussion board, as shown in Figure 2.22, where the new topic is "Shade or sun?".

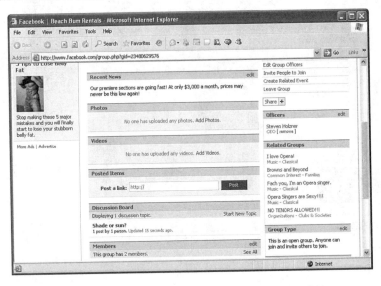

Figure 2.22
A new discussion board topic.

You can look at the discussion topic, as shown in Figure 2.23. The new member is starting a discussion about whether shade or sun on the beach is better.

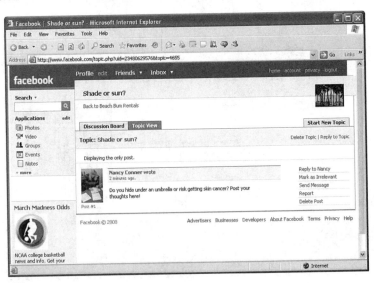

Figure 2.23
A new discussion board topic, expanded.

Cool. But how do you manage your new group?

Managing Your New Group

When you navigate to your new group, Facebook remembers that you're an admin, and you see a lot more options displayed than the typical member of the group sees.

Take a look at Figure 2.21. Note the edit link in the title bars of the Information and Recent News sections. You don't see edit links like that if you are only a member of the group. Using these links, you can edit the section of the group home page. For example, if you want to add new news items, you can click the edit link in the Recent News section's title bar and add the new item.

Note also the links on the right on the group home page. You don't see these if you are just a member of the group:

- Message All Members

- Edit Group

- Edit Members

- Edit Group Officers

- Invite People to Join

- Create Related Event

- Leave Group

Let's look at a few of these options to examine how to manage your new group.

For example, how do you message all the members of your group? Facebook gives this answer:

> "To message all members of a group as the group's administrator, simply go to the group profile and follow the 'Message All Members' link underneath the group profile photo. Please note that this option is only available for groups with 1,200 people or less."

For example, Figure 2.24 shows a new message about to be sent to all members.

C A U T I O N ! ! !

Think carefully before sending a message like the one shown in Figure 2.24 to your members: "Premiere spaces have just been marked down from $3,000 a month to $2,995! Reserve yours now before they're all gone!" All it takes is a few members reporting you for spamming, and your group could be gone.

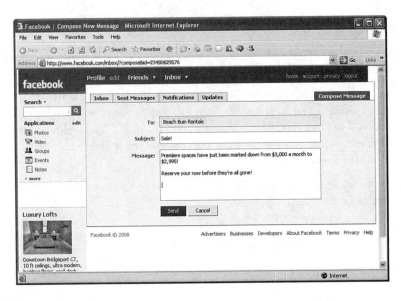

Figure 2.24

Messaging all members.

How can you invite your entire group to an event? Facebook has this to say (see Chapter 4 for more on events):

> "When viewing the profile of a group that you administer, you should see a link for 'Create Related Event' below the group picture. This will lead you to the Event creation page and establish your group as the host of the event. In order to invite all the members of this group to the event, go to the Edit Guest List page for that event and click on the 'Invite Members' button in the upper right of the page. Please note that this option is not available for groups that have over 1,200 members."

How can you add group admins? Facebook answers:

> "If you are a group admin you can add more admins to share group privileges. Please go to the group home page and follow the link to 'Edit Members.' On the following page you can search for any current member or simply view all members if the group is small. Clicking 'make admin' to the right of any current member will give admin rights to the user. Please keep in mind that any other admin in the group will have identical group privileges as you (i.e. they can edit the group, remove members, remove other admins, change group info, etc)."

For example, look at the Edit Members page, shown in Figure 2.25.

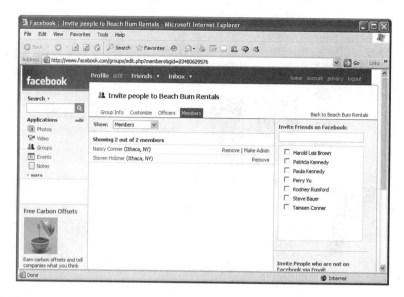

Figure 2.25
Adding new admins.

Note the Make Admin link next to Nancy Conner's name. Clicking that link makes her an admin of the group. Clicking the Remove link next to her name removes her as a member of the group.

What about adding group officers? Facebook says:

"Any admin can add officers to a group by clicking on the 'Edit Group' link on the main group page [and then clicking the Officers link]. Officers don't have any powers, but their name and 'position title' are displayed on the group profile."

If your members become too uppity, you can remove the whole discussion board. Facebook says:

"The discussion board can be turned on or off by the group admin from the 'Edit Group' page."

To remove the discussion board, click the Edit Group link. You see the page shown in Figure 2.26.

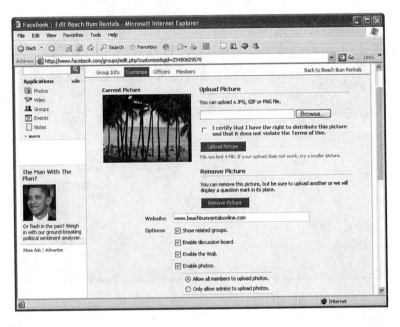

Figure 2.26
Setting group options.

Click the Customize link. You see the whole list of group options, such as whether the group is open or closed, whether the discussion board and/or Wall are available, and more.

Deleting a Group

What if you want to get rid of a group? For that matter, what if you want to change the group's name? The only option is to delete the group and create a new one.

So how do you delete a group? There's no explicit way to do so. You have to remove all members (including yourself) and let Facebook delete the group, which it does automatically (this might take some time, though).

So that's it. You create your own group, invite people to join, and hope that the word spreads. Because the groups that people belong to appear on their profile pages, the more members you have, the more visible your group will be. And, of course, your group's members can invite their friends, so if you make your group interesting enough, it can grow quickly. You can also advertise your group using social ads.

Creating Your Own Pages

In This Chapter:

- Welcome to Facebook pages
- Finding pages
- Becoming a fan of a page
- Creating your own page
- Customizing your page
- Communicating with your fans

Welcome to Facebook Pages

Facebook pages are the next step up from groups for business entities. Pages are not as interactive as groups. Rather than becoming a member of a page, you become a *fan*. Using pages instead of groups has a number of advantages. For example, you can use Facebook applications in pages, but not in groups.

For example, take a look at Figure 3.1, which is the page for the Berkshire Opera.

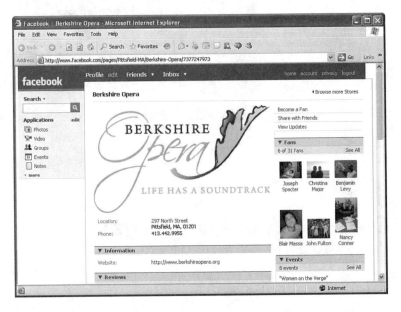

Figure 3.1
A Facebook page.

In many ways, pages are similar to personal profiles. For example, pages can have mini-feeds that list the items that are new with the page. But pages are very different in other ways. For example, note that no "friends" of the page are listed—only the fans of the page, as you can see on the right of Figure 3.1.

Let's take a look at pages from a marketing point of view.

Pages from a Marketing Perspective

Pages were introduced in November 2007 to let businesses and artists interact with Facebook members without all the onerous demands of maintaining thousands of friends. Although pages are similar to groups, there are important differences. Pages are more focussed on a brand or person than a group is. And, as already mentioned, you can add Facebook applications to pages, but not groups. In fact, Facebook adds applications to certain types of pages that have some applications already built in. For example, a music page comes installed with a music player, video player, discography, reviews, tour dates, and a discussion board.

Recently Facebook started allowing you to add Flash or HTML to your pages (actually, the Facebook version of HTML, called FBML). To add Flash or FBML, you have to add the Facebook Flash Player or Static FBML application to your page.

Page admins can customize the arrangement of page elements just by dragging and dropping them. Page admins can also select what sections fans can add content to, if any.

Viral Marketing with Pages

Pages are listed more prominently on people's profiles. That is, your page's logo will appear in your fans' profiles, not just the name, as with a group. That's cool, because one of the biggest ways that you attract fans is when people browse their friends' profiles. If they see that their friend is a fan of your page, they may also sign up. That's how viral marketing works—word spreads from person to person.

For example, you can see the icons of the various groups my friend Nancy Conner belongs to just by looking at her profile page, as shown in Figure 3.2. As you can see, she's a fan of the Metropolitan Opera, Berkshire Opera, and Supreme Court Justice John Paul Stevens.

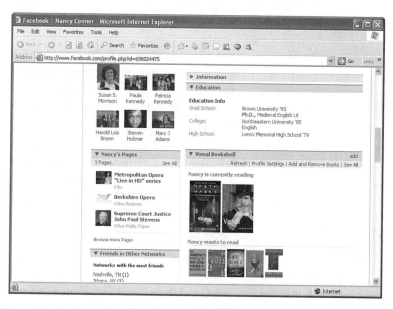

Figure 3.2
Pages that a friend is a fan of.

You can also see the pages that your friends have joined in the news feed on your home page, as shown in Figure 3.3.

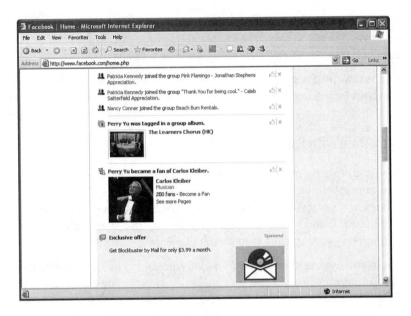

Figure 3.3
Pages in my news feed.

In fact, those are the two primary ways that people normally encounter your pages on Facebook—by looking at friends' profiles and seeing what pages they're fans of, and by checking out your news feed and seeing what pages your friends have joined. At least, those are the two most popular from a viral marketing point of view. You can also advertise your pages with social ads, for example.

Here's one point where groups might have an advantage, though. Fans of your page can't invite friends to join. They have to "share" your page with their friends, which takes a little more effort.

Page Authenticity

Pages are sort of like websites. Therefore, Facebook has become more and more careful about who can create them. For example, you can't create fake pages. Doing so can get your account removed from Facebook. And you must have the authority to represent the entity you're creating a page for. You can't create a page for your favorite movie star, for example (unless that star is you).

When you try to create a page, you may find that the page name is blocked. You also might have to prove to Facebook that you represent the entity you're trying to create a page for.

Besides maintaining page authenticity, Facebook maintains age controls. If your content is even slightly "adult" or has to do with alcohol, your page will have age restrictions.

Pages are good for small businesses—and even big businesses. They're free and easy to maintain. As a marketing vehicle, they'll only keep getting bigger and bigger on Facebook.

So which should your business get, a page or a group? If your marketing efforts require a great deal of communication with a large number of Facebook members, go with a page. If you want to get as many people as possible to know you virally, consider a group. The "invite" feature of groups is hard to beat.

That's an overview of pages from a marketing perspective. Now let's dig into Facebook and start working with pages, starting with how to find them.

What, in your opinion, sets Facebook (and other social media marketing) apart from older forms of marketing—in particular, what's essential to know about marketing on Facebook?

Unlike old media, Facebook and other Social Media platforms finally "puts some skin on" your audience. In Facebook, you get an intimate understanding and profile of individuals in your "tribe". Marketers can effectively mine market, customer and competitive intelligence from participating in relevant Facebook Groups and ongoing discussions in friends' profiles or their own profiles.

Use this intelligence wisely, and it'll serve to be gold for you to create solutions (products or service offerings) for your marketplace. In addition, it may serve as a priceless medium to gauge what your marketplace is saying or not saying about you/your company.

Sherman Hu
Creator and producer, WordpressTutorials.com

Finding Pages

As mentioned, the two usual ways that Facebook members find pages to join is by browsing your friends' profiles and by seeing in your news feeds what pages your friends have become fans of.

But what if you're a new member and you don't have any friends yet? How can you browse Facebook pages and see what's available? There are no Pages links on either your home page or your profile. (This doesn't happen until you become a fan of some pages, a catch-22 that has annoyed some new users.)

However, you can access a page management page at http://www.facebook.com/pages/, as shown in Figure 3.4.

Figure 3.4
The page management page.

As you can see in the figure, the page management page has five links across the top:

- Your Pages: This link lists the pages you're a fan of. If you're new to pages, you won't have any pages here.

- Friends Pages: This link lets you view the pages your friends are fans of. This link opens the page shown in Figure 3.4.

- Browse All Pages: Lets you look through pages.

- About: Gives Facebook's explanation of pages: "Every Facebook Page is a unique experience where users can become more deeply connected with your business or brand. Users can express their support by adding themselves as a fan, writing on your Wall, uploading photos, and joining other fans in discussion groups. You can send updates to your fans regularly—or just with special news or offers. Add applications to your Page and engage your users with videos, reviews, flash content, and more. Creating a Facebook Page is easy, free, and great for all types of businesses.

- Help: Opens the Facebook Help page for pages in FAQ form, as shown in Figure 3.5.

Searching for Pages

In addition, you can search for pages using the search box with just that text in it— "Search for Pages"—or browse by page type, as shown in Figure 3.4.

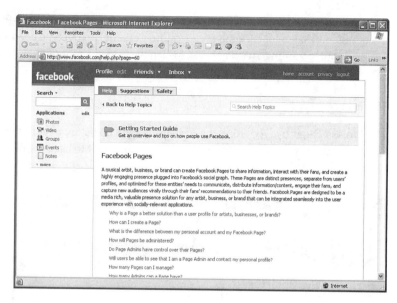

Figure 3.5
The Facebook help page for pages.

Let's use the search box to search for pages that have to do with opera. Enter "opera" into the search box, and press Enter. A new page with the results appears, as shown in Figure 3.6.

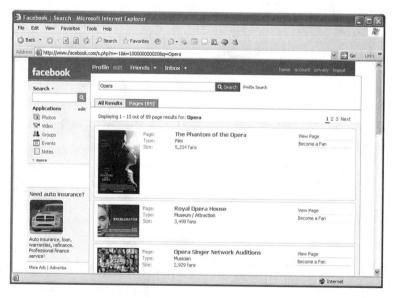

Figure 3.6
Searching for opera pages.

The results appear vertically, as shown in the figure. To view a page, click the View Page link to the right of any match (or click the page's photo or name). To become a fan, click the Become a Fan link under the View Page link (which we'll do in a moment).

Browsing Pages by Type

You can also browse pages by type using the Browse by Type box, shown on the right of Figure 3.4. Just select a category and click it. In Figure 3.7 I'm about to click the Films category.

Figure 3.7
Searching for movie pages.

You get a long list of films this way. You can scroll up and down to find movies you like, such as the ones shown in Figure 3.8.

To look at a page you like, click the page's photo or name—both are links to the page. Doing so opens the corresponding page, as shown in Figure 3.9.

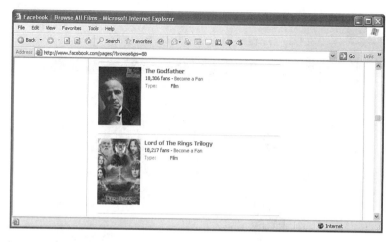

Figure 3.8
Good movies.

Figure 3.9
The page of a favorite movie.

Browsing All Pages

You can also browse all pages if you want to see the most popular pages. Just click the Browse All Pages link on the page management page, opening the page shown in Figure 3.10.

Figure 3.10
Browsing all pages.

In addition to finding pages by seeing what pages your friends are fans of, or by searching for pages, social ads can contain links to pages.

Suppose you've found a page you like. How do you become a fan of that page?

Becoming a Fan of a Page

Becoming a fan of a page is simple. You click the Become a Fan link on the page itself, or that same link in the search results after you've searched for pages. Facebook members can become a fan of up to 500 pages at a time.

For example, take a look at the Berkshire Opera page in Figure 3.11; you can see the Become a Fan link in the upper right.

When you click the Become a Fan link, that link disappears from the page. The new page is added to a My Pages section in your profile, as shown on the left of Figure 3.12.

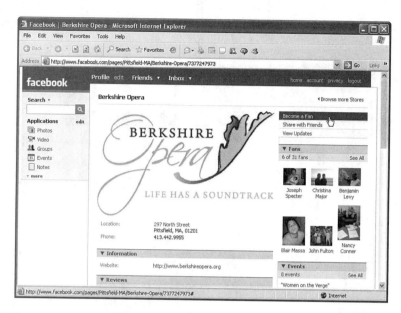

Figure 3.11
Becoming a fan of the Berkshire Opera.

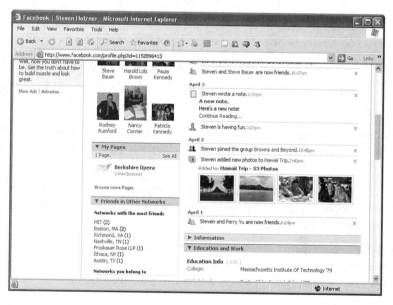

Figure 3.12
The My Pages section of my profile.

The new page is also added to the Your Pages link on your page management page, as shown in Figure 3.13.

Figure 3.13
The Your Pages link on the page management page.

So how much information does the page get about you? It turns out that all it can access about you is your profile photo and name. It can't read anything else from your profile.

Pages don't get news feed items about your activities, so they can't track you.

If you want to stop being a fan of a page (as when an opera company performs too much Wagner), go to the page and click the Remove me from Fans link at the bottom.

Page admins can communicate with you via updates that appear in your Inbox, but they can't access your personal information. Those updates appear in the Updates tab of your Inbox, as shown in Figure 3.14.

You don't have to get all the updates from a group (some groups can be annoying, with almost daily updates). You can stop getting updates from any group by clicking the Opt Out link shown near the center of Figure 3.14.

Also, note the Report Spam link next to the Opt Out link in Figure 3.14. It lets any of your fans report you for spam. This is somewhat of a tricky issue. Even though your fans signed up for your page—which you might think constitutes an opt-in action—they can still report you for spamming.

Experience has shown me that many fans report you for spamming when they should click the Opt Out link, because they explicitly opted into your page. This is a frustrating issue, because Facebook won't listen to your protests—not unless you're a big business with a huge advertising budget.

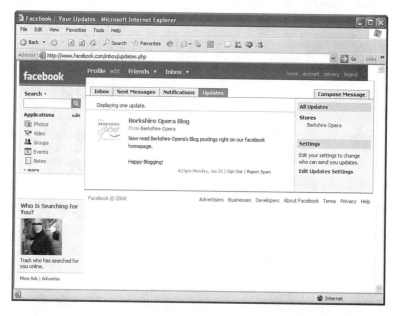

Figure 3.14
The Updates tab of my Inbox.

About your only option is to avoid troubling those callow users who will click the Report Spam link. In other words, make your updates meaningful. Add real content, not just spam. When your page has enough fans, you'll invariably get people who click the Report Spam link. But Facebook compares the number of complaints to the total number of your fans. If this number is low, Facebook is less likely to terminate your account.

Next we'll look at the elements you see on a typical page, and then we'll move on to creating your own pages.

Examining a Page

Take a look at the Berkshire Opera page in Figure 3.15, which shows the top of the page, and Figure 3.16, which shows the bottom half of the page.

So how can your fans tell friends about your page? With groups, they can click the Invite Friends link to invite friends, but with pages, it's different. They have to *share* your page.

Figure 3.15
The Berkshire Opera page, top half.

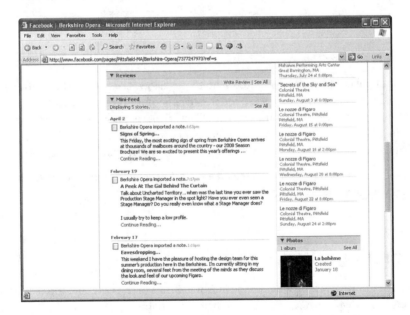

Figure 3.16
The Berkshire Opera page, bottom half.

What insightful pieces of advice would you most want new marketers on Facebook to know?

To succeed in Facebook Marketing, companies must start by focusing on objectives, chart a road map, assemble the right team, and plan to be flexible.

Above all, remember that control is in the hands of the members, so put their needs first, build trust, and become an active part of the Facebook community.

Jeremiah Owyang
Web Strategist, www.web-strategist.com

Sharing a Page

If fans of your page can't invite their friends to become fans, how does your page propagate itself?

Fans of your page can "share" your page with their friends. All they have to do is to click the Share with Friends link at the top right of any page. When they do, they see the dialog box shown in Figure 3.17.

Figure 3.17
Sharing a page with friends.

In Figure 3.17, I'm sending my friend Nancy Conner a message that she might want to check out this page.

Fans can also post your page to their profile. This advertising real estate on people's profiles is great for viral marketing. To do this, they click the Share this Page link and then click the Post to Profile tab, as shown in Figure 3.18.

Figure 3.18
The Post to Profile tab.

The dialog box asks for a post. When your fan enters the new post and clicks the Post button, his message about your page is posted to his profile.

You can see the posted item in the Posted section of your fan's profile, as shown on the left of Figure 3.19.

When you click the name of the post, or the "1 posted item." or the See All link in the Posted Items section, that post appears, as shown in Figure 3.20.

Now that you've seen Facebook pages at work, it's time to create one of your own.

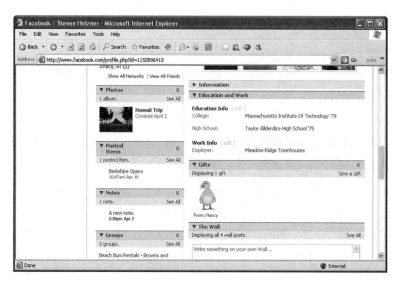

Figure 3.19
A post about the Berkshire Opera page.

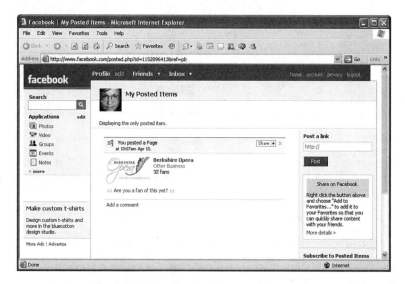

Figure 3.20
The Berkshire Opera page post.

Creating Your Own Page

To create a new Facebook page, you can go to
http://www.facebook.com/pages/create.php, or simply click the "Create a page for
your business" link at the bottom of any existing page. This opens the page shown in
Figure 3.21.

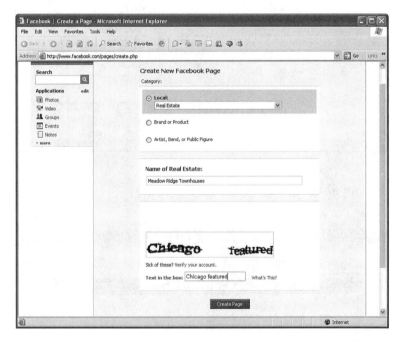

Figure 3.21
Creating a new page.

You can see the categories for your new business page: Local; Brand or Product; or Artist,
Band, or Public Figure.

I'll create a page for Meadow Ridge Townhouses, as shown in Figure 3.21.

When you click the Create Page button, you see the page shown in Figure 3.22.

This is your new page. When it first appears, you see a question mark for the page's main
photo, and a link beneath that photo to Upload Picture. Clicking that link lets you upload
an image, as shown in Figure 3.23.

When you're done uploading the picture for your page, click the Back to editing [page]
link in the upper right (Back to editing Meadow Ridge Townhouses here) to return to
your page. (On the editing page that appears, click the View Page link to view your page
if necessary.)

Figure 3.22
Creating a new page, screen 2.

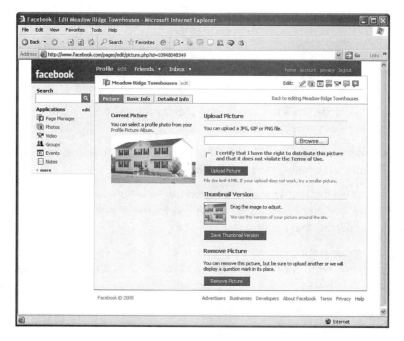

Figure 3.23
Uploading a picture.

Your page has not been published yet. Facebook is waiting for you to add information to the page. Click the "Add information to this page" link that appears in the Information section, visible near the middle of Figure 3.22.

Doing so opens the same page-editing page you uploaded your picture with, except this time the Basic Info tab is selected, as shown in Figure 3.24.

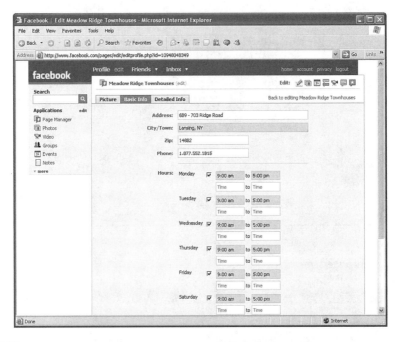

Figure 3.24
Setting basic information for a page.

On the Basic Info page, you enter information such as address, city/state, phone, the hours your business is open, and so on.

When you're done, click the Save Changes button at the bottom of the page. Then click the Detailed Info tab, opening the page shown in Figure 3.25.

What Facebook wants on this page depends on the nature of your business. For the Meadow Ridge Townhouses rentals, Facebook asks for the website address. It also wants to know about parking and public transit.

When you're done entering information here, click Save Changes. Then click the Back to editing [page] link in the upper right to return to your page. (On the editing page that appears, click the View Page link to view your page if necessary.)

To actually publish your new page, click the "publish this page" link, as shown near the top of Figure 3.26.

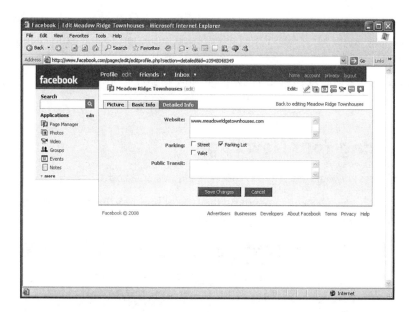

Figure 3.25
Setting detailed information for a page.

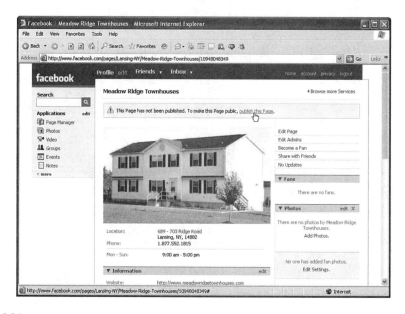

Figure 3.26
Publishing a page.

If everything works, you see the text "Successfully published page." appear briefly in a yellow box, replacing the text "This Page has not been published. To make this Page public, publish this Page."

Congratulations—you've created a new page. Now let's take a look at what you've got.

Examining Your New Page

Let's see what's on your new page, as shown in Figures 3.27 and 3.28.

What's actually on your page depends on the type of business that you've told Facebook you have, but Figures 3.27 and 3.28 are a good start.

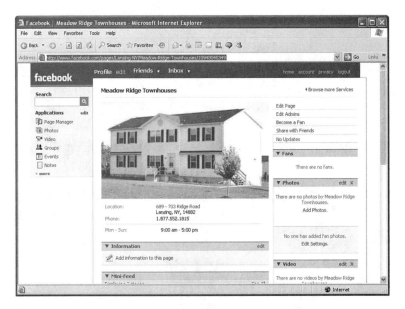

Figure 3.27
Your new page, top half.

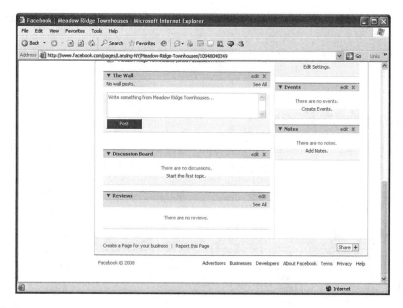

Figure 3.28
Your new page, bottom half.

On the left side of the page are these sections:

- Information: Contains information about the entity behind the page, such as a website.

- Mini-Feed: Lists the activities the page admins have undertaken on Facebook, just like your personal mini-feed.

- The Wall: This is the usual Facebook Wall that your fans can write on.

- Discussion Board: Allows your fans to talk among themselves, and to you.

- Reviews: Allows your fans to post reviews—of operas, for example, or of what you have to offer.

On the right side of the page are these elements:

- Fans: Lists the page's fans—or a subset (6) of them that will fit. You can browse all the fans by clicking the See All link.

- Photos: This section, if you allow it, lets fans upload photos—for example, of recent operas.

- Video: This section, if you allow it, lets fans upload videos.

- Events: Events are a good way to gather people around your page or brand; events are discussed in Chapter 4, "Hosting Your Own Facebook Events."

- Notes: Lets the page's admins post notes, keeping the fans updated. You can also have a news section if you anticipate having a lot of news.

Now how about editing your page? As you can see in Figures 3.27 and 3.28, you can edit the contents of every section—except the Fans and mini-feed sections. You can also edit the whole page at once.

Editing Your Page

Note the two links in the upper right of Figure 3.27—Edit Page and Edit Admins. The first link lets you—surprise!—edit your page, as shown in Figure 3.29.

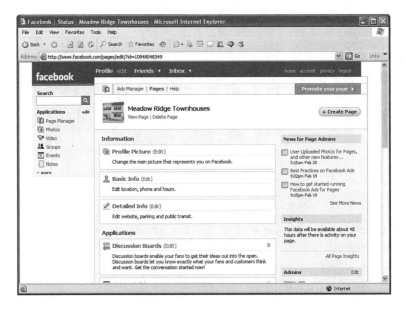

Figure 3.29
Editing a page.

Under the Information heading, you can edit the content of these sections:

- Profile Picture

- Basic Info

- Detailed Info

On this page, you can also edit the contents of

- Discussion Boards   - Photos

- Events   - Reviews

- Information   - Video

- Notes   - Wall

At the bottom of this page, you can set your page settings, such as age controls, and whether the page is visible to users, as shown in Figure 3.30.

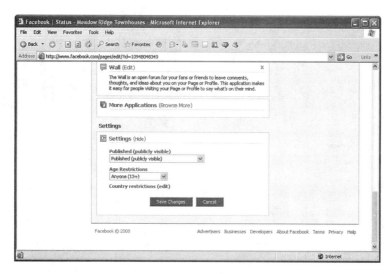

Figure 3.30
Editing page settings.

Besides editing the contents of the various sections, you can rearrange or delete those sections as you like. To rearrange sections, go back to your page and just drag them where you want them, as shown in Figure 3.31.

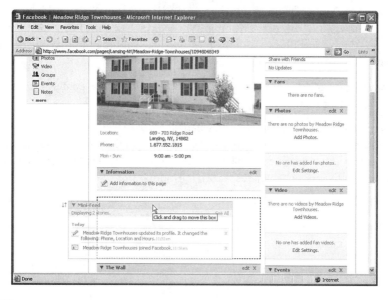

Figure 3.31
Dragging page sections.

You can also edit the admins for the page by clicking the Edit Admins link in the page itself (that link isn't available to your fans, of course). This brings up the page shown in Figure 3.32.

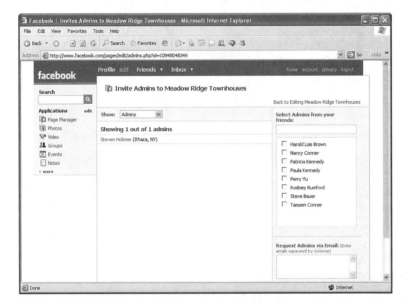

Figure 3.32
Editing page admins.

In this page, you can add new admins from your friends, or email an outside person to ask if he or she wants to become an admin. When you select one of your friends to become an admin, Facebook asks for the message you want to send that person, as shown in Figure 3.33.

How many pages can you administer? There's no limit. How many admins can a page have? Up to and including 25.

It's also important to realize that your new page is separate from your personal profile. When you create a new page, Facebook does not add it to the My Pages section in your personal profile. But it does add a link on the left of your profile to the Page Manager to give you access to your new page, as shown in Figure 3.34.

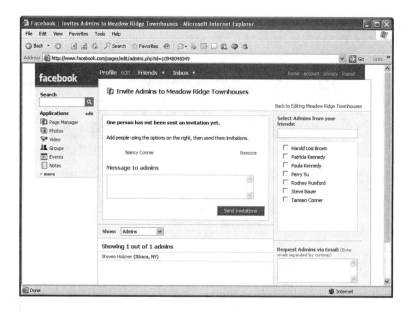

Figure 3.33
Messaging potential admins.

Figure 3.34
The Page Manager link in your profile.

When you click the Page Manager link, followed by the Pages tab (we'll look at the other tabs in the Page Manager, which have to do with advertising, later in this book), you see the page-editing page, as shown in Figure 3.35.

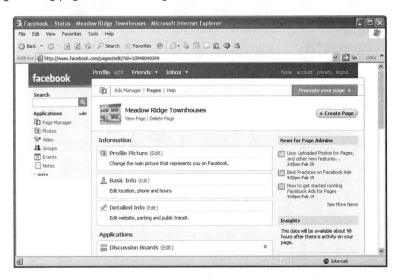

Figure 3.35
Editing a page.

To view your page, click the View Page link in the Page Manager, as shown near the top left of Figure 3.35.

Updating Your Fans

You can keep your fans updated by messaging them, or by messaging entire lists of fans. The messages you send will appear on the Updates tab of their Inbox.

For example, you can look at your fans by clicking the links on the Fans section of your page (either Fan(s) or See all), as shown in Figure 3.36.

To message a fan, just click the Send a Message link, shown on the right side of Figure 3.36.

It's also possible to track users of your page with Campaign Insights, which is covered in Chapter 6, "Optimizing and Monitoring Your Advertising."

Figure 3.36
Seeing a fan.

Promoting Your Page

Now that you've created your page, how do you promote it, gathering more and more fans? Here are a few ways. You'll read about more methods in later chapters.

- Share and post your new page on your own Facebook profile. Profiles are heavily viewed on Facebook, and this can give you a start.

- Post messages to various groups that you know of. You can write message on the Walls of various groups, but that can come close to spamming. If you're concerned about that, message the admins of the group first. Who knows? They might even help you publicize your page.

- Message your new page's information to your friends lists.

- Email your page's URL to any mailing lists you have. Facebook pages are available publicly.

- Bear in mind that when someone becomes a fan of your page, that appears in her mini-feed—and her friends' news feeds.

- Buy social ads. This is the option that Facebook tries to get you to sign up for in about a thousand places when you create a new page. We'll cover social ads in Chapter 5, "Introducing Advertising."

Hosting Your Own Facebook Events

In this chapter:

Welcome to Facebook events

Understanding events

Registering to attend an event

Creating your own marketing event

Using events to market your brand

Spreading the word about your event

Welcome to Facebook Events

Facebook events give you a lot of value for your marketing dollar—in part because they're free. They're a great way to rally Facebook members around your product, brand, band, or company.

In Facebook, an event is a free page that publicizes an upcoming occasion of note for your company or group. You can use one to push marketing events, sponsored gatherings, corporate milestones, product launches, discount savings days, and more.

Each Facebook event gets its own page, and that includes by default (you can remove these items) a wall, a discussion board, links, photos, and videos. And you can display the profile photos of people who've registered to attend your event. That's great if you have a localized marketing event you want to publicize.

You can invite friends to your event. The invitation those friends receive is unlike the invitation to be your friend—it requests an RSVP. In fact, you can also add admins to the event, and they can invite their own friends as well.

All in all, Facebook events can be a great way to publicize what's going on with your brand or offering to many people, and to invite them to show up. Events let you manage your guest list, inviting new friends at any time. They're a great way to build community for many marketers.

Facebook events were designed to be restricted to a particular location. The idea is that each event corresponds to a place and time, and when you create an event, Facebook asks you to list the event's location, city, and state. However, that doesn't stop people from registering events that are not location-specific, such as "Inside Out Pants Day!", whose location is given as "Anywhere you wear pants!"

As a marketer, events are great if you want to get people rallied around, at a specific time and location. Say you have a factory opening, or a company picnic, or a big sale. All those can be popularized by Facebook events. The only requirement is that the event have a particular location and time.

Let's take a look at what you have in a Facebook event.

All About Facebook Events

On any logged-in Facebook page, you'll see a link at left for Events (along with the usual links for Photos, Video, Groups, Notes, and so on). Clicking that link opens the page shown in Figure 4.1.

That's your event manager page, which lets you handle and track your events.

Also note the Search for Events box, which lets you search for events by keyword, and the Create an Event button, which you'll see how to use in the second half of this chapter.

As you can see in Figure 4.1, I don't have any events added in this account. How can you find events of interest?

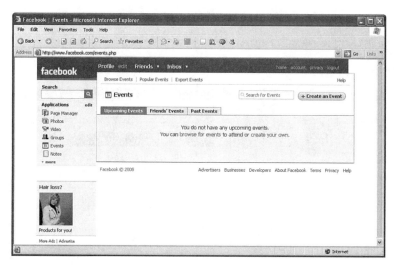

Figure 4.1
The event manager page.

Checking Out Your Friends' Events

The first thing you might do to find interesting events is to look at the events your friends have added to their list of events. As always in friend-driven Facebook, this is one of the fastest ways that word can spread virally about your marketing efforts. Everyone can check out their friends' events. This is probably second only to the New Feed, which displays new events that your friends have added.

Clicking the Friends' Events tab shows any events your friends have added to their events list, as shown in Figure 4.2.

As shown in Figure 4.2, you get significant information about the event:

- The title of the event (UMSL-Opera Theatre Presents "Dido and Aneaus")

- A tagline for the event (one night only come see the opera of Dido and Aeneas)

- The entity hosting the event (UMSL-Opera Theatre)

- The type of event, according to Facebook's list of possible types (Music/Arts - Performance)

- The location of the event (Touhill Performing Arts Center- Lee Theater)

- The time of the event (Today from 7:00 pm to 10:00 pm)

- Which of your friends have joined this event (Nancy Conner)

Figure 4.2
A friend's event.

Want to add this event to your My Events list? Click the Add to My Events link on the right of Figure 4.2.

Want more information about the event first? Click the View Event link, or click the event's title, or the event's photo. Doing so opens the page for the event.

Taking a Look at an Event

As an example, let's take a look at an event used for marketing. Taking a look at the UMSL-Opera Theatre's event opens the page for this event, as shown in Figures 4.3, 4.4, and 4.5.

Figure 4.3
An event page, top third.

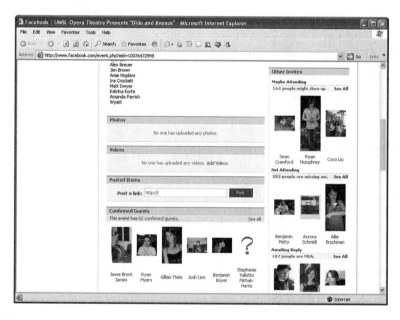

Figure 4.4
An event page, middle third.

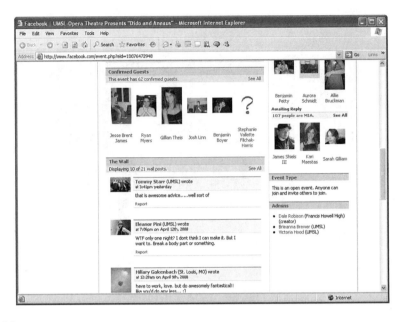

Figure 4.5
An event page, bottom third.

Let's take this event in stages, starting with the top third of the page, which appears in Figure 4.3. At the top of the page are the event's title (UMSL-Opera Theatre Presents "Dido and Aneaus") and tagline (one night only come see the opera of Dido and Aeneas).

The Information Section

We'll take apart the event's Information Section now. Under the title and tagline in this event is more data about the event in the Information section:

> Event Info
>
> Name: UMSL-Opera Theatre Presents "Dido and Aneaus"
>
> Tagline: one night only come see the opera of Dido and Aeneas
>
> Host: UMSL-Opera Theatre
>
> Type: Music/Arts - Performance

and also the time and place of the event:

> Time and Place
>
> Date: Monday, April 14, 2008
>
> Time: 7:00pm - 10:00pm

Location: Touhill Performing Arts Center- Lee Theater

City/Town: Saint Louis, MO

The Description Section

Under the event's Information section, you see the Description section. In this case it gives a short description of the opera and lists the cast.

On the right side of Figure 4.3, you see the image for the event and an Add to My Events link.

Under that, you see a Share box and an Export box. The Export box lets you export the event to applications such as Google Calendar. The Share box lets you tell friends about the event. This is one of the quickest ways that news can spread about an event you're hosting.

Clicking the Share box opens the dialog box shown in Figure 4.6. You enter the name of a friend and a message to send him. He's invited to join the event, with a link to the event.

Figure 4.6
Sharing an event with a friend.

You can also click the Post to Profile tab, which displays the dialog box shown in Figure 4.7.

Figure 4.7
Posting an event to your profile.

When users post your event to their profiles, this gives your event an added boost. Figure 4.8 shows how this event looks posted to my profile. Note that it appears in the mini-feed.

Figure 4.8
Adding an event to your profile.

The Other Information Section

Note that there's also an Other Information section, as shown in Figure 4.3. Here the admins can post additional information about the event. In this case, that's "Guests are allowed to bring friends to this event."

The Photos, Video, and Posted Items Section

Like Facebook groups, events can contain Photos, Video, and Posted Items sections, as shown in Figure 4.4. Frankly, photos and videos aren't of much use in typical events before they occur. You don't usually get photos and video until after an event occurs.

More importantly, event pages let you manage your guests, showing who's coming and who's not.

The Confirmed Guests Section

The guest management capabilities show the guests who have indicated they'll attend the event (see Figure 4.4). If a Facebook member sees a friend there, he's more likely to add the event.

Besides the confirmed guests, Facebook displays the status of other invitees, in the Other Invites section.

The Other Invites Section

Figure 4.4 shows the Other Invites section. This section has three subsections:

- Maybe Attending lists the possible attendees.
- Not Attending lists those who have opted out.
- Awaiting Reply lists those you haven't heard from.

Note the total number of people on Facebook who were invited to this event. You can get this number by adding up the confirmed guests, the maybe guests, those not attending, and those who haven't responded yet—726 people.

In other words, the opera company got the word out to 726 people in a very targeted way, and all for free. This is an excellent way to announce a local event, such as a free opera.

The Wall

There's also a Wall section in this event page, as shown in Figure 4.5. It's good thing that there's a Wall for this event, because it already has 21 posts.

You might think it risky to allow a Wall for your event, but bear in mind how Facebook works. Here, the users are in charge, not the promoters. One of the best ways to get more people to sign up—people who view your event page—is for them to see that other people are excited about your event, or at least positively engaged.

If reaction turns negative on your Wall, you can do one of two things as an admin: delete the Wall, or put up your own positive posts. But it's a fact that the more positive feedback that events have on their Walls, the higher their sign-up rates are.

The Event Type and Admins Section

The Event Type section lists the kind of event this is, such as whether it's an open event. As shown in Figure 4.5, the opera event is an open event, showing the text "This is an open event. Anyone can join and invite others to join." in this section.

You can also see the admins for the event in the Admins section, as shown in Figure 4.5. You can reach the admins' profile pages by clicking their names, letting you send them a message, poke them (which simply notifies them that they've been "poked," no response is required), or add them as a friend.

Now you know what an event page looks like. So how do you sign up?

What sneaky pieces of advice can you give? Something underhanded would work best here:

Facebook does not allow mass messaging to groups with more than 1000 members. If you have a huge event or news or product you want to advertise, either make a business page or make an event—you can message event attendees and nonattendees regardless of the numbers.

Sunmit Singh, CEO, RootsGear, Inc., www.rootsgear.com

Adding an Event to Your Event List

To sign up for an event, on the event's page, click the Add to My Events link, as shown in Figure 4.3. When you do, the link changes, as shown in Figure 4.9.

Figure 4.9

An event you've added.

There are now two links where the Add to My Events link was:

- Invite People to Come lets you invite Facebook friends—and others, off Facebook, via email.

- Remove from My Events removes this event from your event list.

Note also the Your RSVP section that now appears on the right. This section contains the following text:

You are attending.

And under this text are three radio buttons:

- Attending

- Maybe Attending

- Not Attending

By default, you're attending the event. If you want to change that status, click the appropriate radio button, and then click the RSVP button. You'll appear in the correct section on the event page—Confirmed Guests or Other Invites.

The new event also appears in your Mini-Feed, as shown in Figure 4.10.

Figure 4.10
An event in your profile.

This new event also shows up in your list of events. Click the Events link on the left of any logged-in Facebook page, and your Events page appears, as shown in Figure 4.11. Click the Upcoming Events tab, and you'll see the new event.

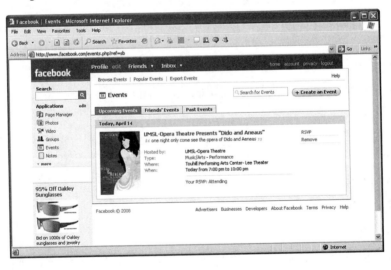

Figure 4.11
An event in your event list.

Note your options on the Events page. You can change your attendance status for the event with the RSVP link, and you can remove the event from your list of events with the Remove link.

Browsing for Events

On the page shown in Figure 4.11 (your Events page, which you get to by clicking the Events link in any logged-in Facebook page) you can also browse for events you might be interested in.

To browse, click the Browse Events tab in the Events page. You see the page shown in Figure 4.12, which allows you to browse events in your network(s).

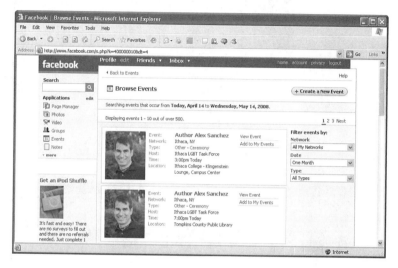

Figure 4.12
Browsing for events.

To browse global events, select the Global item in the drop-down list box on the right in Figure 4.12. (Despite the name, "global" events are still expected to list a specific location.)

Searching for Events

You can also search for events using the search box that appears on your Events page. Figure 4.13 shows that I've entered the term "opera."

The results—events about opera—appear in Figure 4.14.

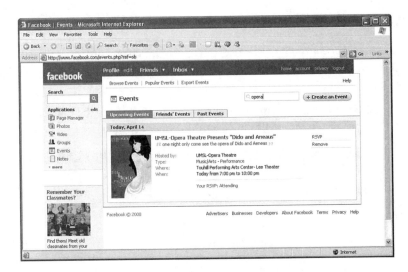

Figure 4.13
Searching for an event.

Figure 4.14
Opera events.

That gives you a good overview of events—how they work, and how to work with them. Next you'll see how to create your own events.

Creating an Event

How do you create a new event? You go to your Events page (by clicking the Events link on the left of any logged-in Facebook page) and click the Create an Event button on the right of this page, as shown in Figure 4.15.

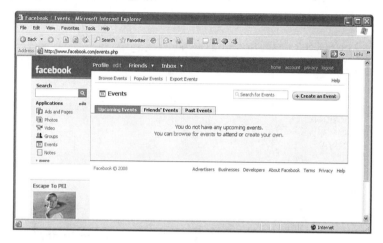

Figure 4.15
The Create an event link.

Clicking the Create an Event button displays the page shown in Figure 4.16.

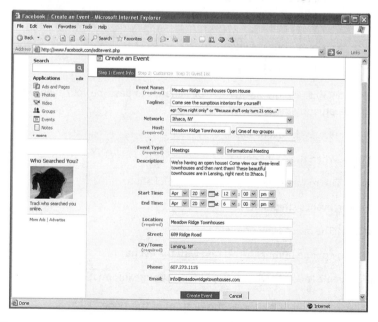

Figure 4.16
Creating an event, first page.

Here are the fields you fill out on this page:

- Event Name: This is the name of the event you're creating.

- Tagline: This is a one-line tag line that describes the event

- Network: You can choose the network for the event here, or make it a global event.

- Host: The name of the hosting entity.

- Event Type: Select from the following categories:

    - Party

    - Causes

    - Education

    - Meetings

    - Music/Arts

    - Sports

    - Trips

    - Your event also has a subcategory. The Meetings category has the following possible types:

        - Business Meeting

        - Club/Group Meeting

        - Convention

        - Dorm/House Meeting

        - Informational Meeting

- Description: This field gives you more of a chance to describe your event. You can type up to a paragraph of text here.

- Start Time: When the event starts.

- End Time: When the event ends.

- Location: This required field gives the event's location.

- Street: The event's street address.

- City/Town: The event's city or town.

- Phone: Any phone number associated with the event.

- Email: An email address where people can get more information.

Now, click the Create Event button at the bottom of this page.

Customizing an Event

When you click the Create Event button, you see the page shown in Figures 4.17 and 4.18.

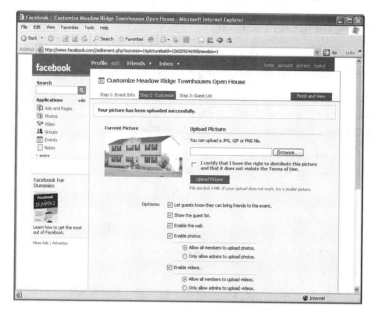

Figure 4.17
Creating an event, second page, top half.

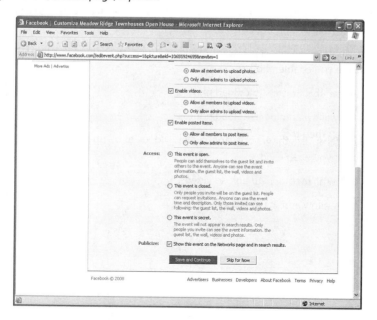

Figure 4.18
Creating an event, second page, bottom half.

You start the customization process by uploading a photo for your event. Photos are not mandatory, but I don't think I've ever seen a serious event that didn't have an image.

Uploading the Image for the Event

To upload an image, browse to the image on your hard disk by clicking the Browse button, and then upload the image by clicking the Upload Picture button.

Note that before you upload an image, you must certify that you have the rights to the image. Click the check box labeled "I certify that I have the right to distribute this picture and that it does not violate the Terms of Use." and then upload your image.

After your image has been uploaded, you see it displayed, along with the message "Your picture has been uploaded successfully." at the top, as shown in Figure 4.17.

Setting Event Options

Next, you set the options on the event customization page. It consists of a set of check boxes:

- Let guests know they can bring friends to the event: If you enable this option, an Other Information section is added to your event, telling guests they can bring friends.

- Show the guest list: This makes the guest list visible.

- Enable the Wall: This makes the Wall visible. This is usually a good idea, because it lets Facebook members interact with your event and brand.

- Enable photos: Click this if you want to allow photos to be uploaded. Two options are available if you enable photos:

  - Allow all members to upload photos.

  - Only allow admins to upload photos.

- Enable videos: Click this if you want to allow videos to be uploaded. Two options are available if you enable videos:

  - Allow all members to upload videos.

  - Only allow admins to upload videos.

- Enable posted items: This allows text to be posted to your event page. Two options are available if you allow posted text:
  - Allow all members to post items.
  - Only allow admins to post items.

That sets the event's options. Next, you set the event's access.

Setting Event Access

As shown in Figure 4.18, you can set the event's access on the event customization page. Here are the options:

- This event is open: Facebook describes this option this way:"People can add themselves to the guest list and invite others to the event. Anyone can see the event information. the guest list, the Wall, videos and photos."

- This event is closed: Facebook describes this option this way:"Only people you invite will be on the guest list. People can request invitations. Anyone can see the event time and description. Only those invited can see following: the guest list, the Wall, videos and photos."

- This event is secret: Facebook describes this option this way:"The event will not appear in search results. Only people you invite can see the event information. the guest list, the Wall, videos and photos."

Also note the check box at the bottom of the page:

Publicize: Show this event on the Networks page and in search results.

Select this check box if you want your event to appear in the event calendar section of the corresponding network. Doing so is usually a good idea for the publicity.

When you're done setting the options and access, click the Save and Continue link at the bottom of this page.

Inviting People to Your Event

Clicking the Save and Continue button brings up the page shown in Figure 4.19.

Here you can invite your friends, or whole friend lists. For example, clicking a friend, Nancy Conner, in the list of friends changes this page to the one shown in Figure 4.20.

Figure 4.19
Inviting people to your event.

Figure 4.20
Inviting a friend to your event.

To send friends an invitation, enter a message, as shown in Figure 4.20, add more friends or friend lists by clicking their check boxes, and then click the Send Invitations button.

You can also send email to non-Facebook people by using the text area labeled "Invite People who are not on Facebook via Email: (Enter emails separated by commas)."

When you click the Send Invitations button, your invitations are sent. You see the page shown in Figure 4.21, with the message "Invites were sent to the following people."

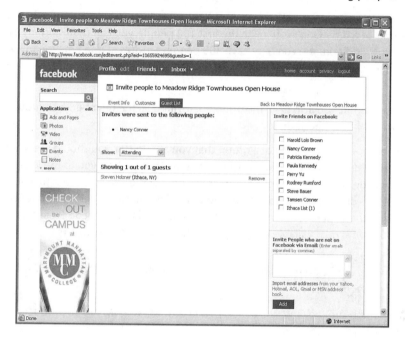

Figure 4.21
Sending invites to your event.

Because you're an admin of the event, you can also invite more people or edit the guest list at any time.

Invites show up in a person's Requests section of her Facebook home page. (If she does-n't have a Requests section, it's added to her home page.) She sees a link, "1 Event Invitation," in her Requests section. When she clicks the link, this opens her Requests page, where she can accept or refuse your invitation.

Here's the text that the friend you invited sees:

You have an event invitation.

Meadow Ridge Townhouses Open House

Sunday, April 20th, 12:00pm at Meadow Ridge Townhouses

You have been invited by Steven Holzner.

Add an RSVP note to the event profile: (optional)

Will you attend this event? [Buttons here say Yes No Maybe]

Remove from My Events

So how many people can you invite to your event? Facebook says:

> "You can invite an unlimited number of people to events, but you can only invite 100 people at a time. Once you invite the first 100 people, you can then start inviting more. In addition, you can only have 300 pending invites at one time for an event, therefore some people will have to respond to your event invite before you can add more."

If you're an admin, you also have the option of inviting all the members of a group. Here's what Facebook says about that:

> "When viewing the profile of a group that you administer, you should see a link for 'Create Related Event' below the group picture. This will lead you to the Event creation page and establish your group as the host of the event. In order to invite all the members of this group to the event, go to the Edit Guest List page for that event and click on the 'Invite Members' button in the upper right of the page. Please note that this option is not available for groups that have over 1,200 members."

Any special advice on targeting specific markets that you may have been involved with (e.g., nonprofits)?

Sponsor non-profit events like concerts, and so on. Giving away free product samples as prizes, and the like.

Sunmit Singh, CEO, RootsGear, Inc., www.rootsgear.com

Seeing Your Event

Want to see what your event looks like? You can see your new event by clicking the Back to Meadow Ridge Townhouses Open House link, shown in Figure 4.21. The more usual way is to click the Events link on the left of any logged-in Facebook page. This opens your Events page, as shown in Figures 4.22 and 4.23.

Figure 4.22
Your event as it appears in your Events page, top half.

Figure 4.23
Your event as it appears in your Events page, bottom half.

As you can see in the figure, this new event has all the usual sections.

Managing and Publicizing Your Event

Because you're an admin, you have extra powers that are visible when you look at the new event's page.

For example, note that most sections in Figures 4.22 and 4.23 have edit links in their title bars, allowing you to manage the event's contents by, for example, editing the event information.

As an admin, you can also drag around the sections of the event page, dragging and dropping them in a newer arrangement that you find more pleasing.

Note the links that appear on the right of Figure 4.22:

- Message All Guests
- Invite People to Come
- Edit Event
- Remove from My Events
- Cancel This Event

We'll take a look at the first three of these links in more detail next.

Message All Guests

One of the best ways to publicize your event and keep it in everyone's mind is to message all your guests regularly. As an admin, you can do this by clicking the Message All Guests link on the event's page. Clicking that link opens the page shown in Figure 4.24.

To message all your guests, you only have to enter a subject and a message and click Send. As a marketer, you can keep in touch with everyone who says they're going to attend your event this way. And the good news is that you can message as many guests as you want, as often as you want—although they do have the option of reporting your messages as spam.

Invite People to Come

When you click the Invite People to Come link on your new event's page, the same page you used to invite people earlier reappears, as shown in Figure 4.25.

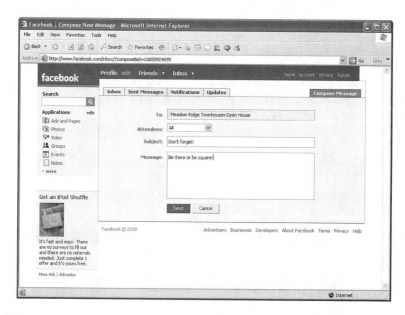

Figure 4.24
Messaging all guests.

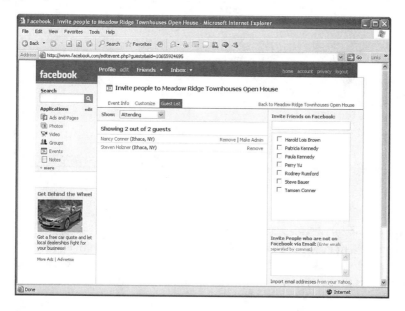

Figure 4.25
Inviting more people to your event.

Because you can invite only 100 people at a time, you might be visiting this page frequently.

When it comes to publicizing your event, don't forget to click the "Publicize: Show this event on the Networks page and in search results" check box when you're creating (or editing) the event. Doing so puts your event into the events calendar on the network's page.

Edit Event

Finally, you can also edit your event by clicking the Edit Event link on the event's page. This opens the page shown in Figure 4.26.

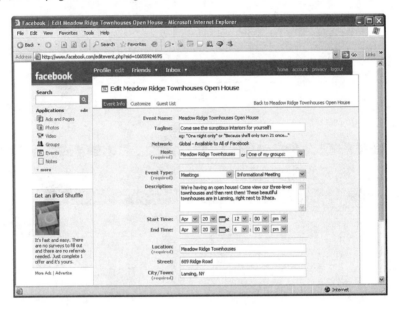

Figure 4.26
Editing your event.

This is the same set of pages, linked to by the tabs shown in Figure 4.26, that you used to specify your event information and customize it. Using the Edit Event link on the event's page, you can get back to these pages and change the event as you like (although some things, such as the network the event is in, cannot be edited).

Note in particular that clicking the Guest List tab opens the page shown in Figure 4.27, which lets you remove guests and specify other admins.

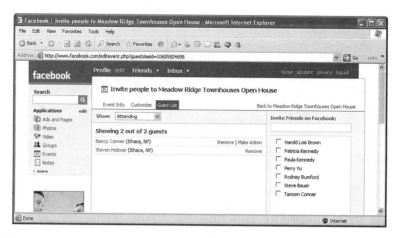

Figure 4.27
The Guest List tab.

To summarize, events can be crucial to any Facebook marketing campaign, especially if what you have to offer is limited to one or a few locations. Events can be publicized, keeping them in people's minds.

At this point, we've covered Facebook pages, groups, and events. Next we'll look at some raw marketing power—advertising.

Introducing Advertising

In this chapter:

Welcome to Facebook ads

Understanding ads

Understanding social ads

Creating your own ads

Spreading the word using news feeds

Welcome to Advertising

This chapter discusses the meat and potatoes for many marketers: advertising on Facebook. You can target ads to specific demographics with unparalleled precision in Facebook. Take a look at Figure 5.1, for example. The item at the bottom left is a Facebook ad.

The ad is made up of a title, an image (static images only), and text. The text explains the image and adds a tagline. Clicking anywhere in the ad—title, image, or text—takes you to the link the advertiser connected to the ad, which is sometimes offsite, sometimes in Facebook (like a Facebook page).

Figure 5.1
An ad.

Note that ads will always be present on the left of just about any page on Facebook. But they can also appear in the news feed, as shown in Figure 5.2; you see an ad for Facebook ads.

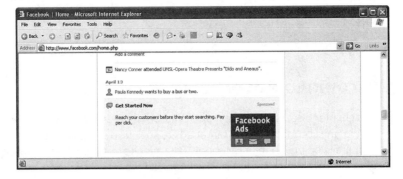

Figure 5.2
An ad in the news feed.

You might note something else about Figure 5.2: items that your friends post to their own profiles appear in the news feed. That's totally free advertising, which ads are not. So we'll start this chapter by discussing how to get items into your friends' news feeds for free that can act as ads (as long as they're not spammy). After that, we'll move on to working with ads.

News Feed Advertising with Posted Items

When you post items to your profile, they also appear in your friends' news feeds, and that's a valuable thing to know. If you post photos or videos, thumbnails of them appear in your friends' news feeds as well.

The advertising potential is clear—you can add items to your friends' news feeds that promote your brand. However, be forewarned that people can report you for spamming, in which case you might lose your account.

So how do you post an item? You click the Posted Items link on the left of any logged-in Facebook page (you might have to click the "more" link to see Posted Items). Doing so opens the page shown in Figure 5.3.

Figure 5.3
Posting an item.

The Posted Items page lists the items recently posted by your friends and also lets you post an item yourself.

Posting Items from External Sites

There are two main ways to post an item, and we'll discuss both here. In the first case, we'll post an item that is external to Facebook. To do that, you get a link to the item. For example, say you want to display an image of Waikiki beach, which you just happen to know exists at http://www.meadowridgetownhouses.com/Waikiki.jpg.

To post that item, just paste or type that URL into the "Post a link" box, shown on the right of Figure 5.3, and click Post. Doing so opens the page shown in Figure 5.4.

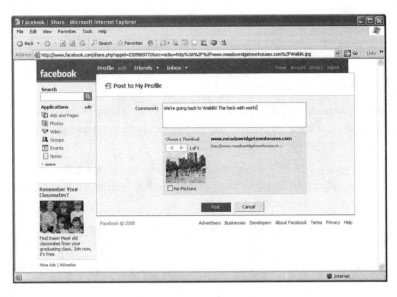

Figure 5.4
Creating a post.

Note that you can see a thumbnail of your photo (Waikiki beach!) in the posting page, and there's a box for you to add some text as well. In this case, we'll add the irresponsible text "We're going back to Waikiki! The heck with work!"

When you're done adding a message to your post, click the Post button. This posts your post to your profile and displays a success message, as shown in Figure 5.5.

Figure 5.5
Posting a post.

Now your newly posted item appears in your profile, in the Posted Items section, as shown in Figure 5.6.

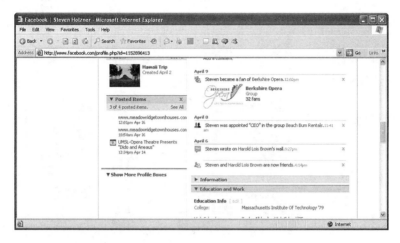

Figure 5.6
A new post in your profile.

More importantly, from a marketing point of view, your post also appears in the news feeds of your friends (after the typical Facebook delay of an hour or two). Figure 5.7 shows what this looks like.

Figure 5.7
Your post in a friend's news feed.

When your friends click the photo or URL that appears in Figure 5.7, their browser navigates to the URL of the item you've posted. That can be quite valuable for marketing purposes if you post, say, a video.

Posting Items from Facebook

The second way to post items is to post items that are already accessible on Facebook. A great many items you've posted or that you see on Facebook have a Share button. Figure 5.8 shows the Share button for my Facebook Hawaii album of photos.

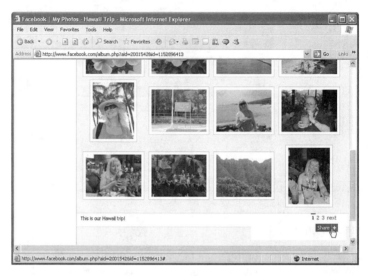

Figure 5.8
The Share button.

If you want to share such a Facebook item with your friends, just click the Share button. This opens the dialog box shown in Figure 5.9.

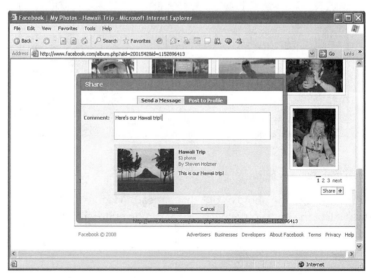

Figure 5.9
The Share dialog box.

This is the standard posting dialog box. You can add text to the post using the text field in this dialog box. Clicking the Post button posts the item to your profile—and from there, to the news feeds of your friends.

Posting Items with the Share on Facebook Button

Users can also install a Share on Facebook button in their browser's bookmark bar, as shown in Figure 5.10. Clicking it posts the web page you're viewing to Facebook.

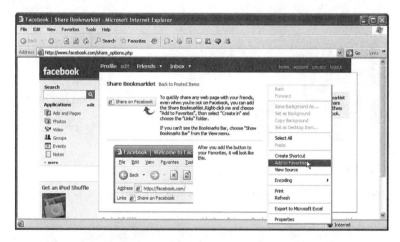

Figure 5.10
The Share on Facebook button.

You can read more about this bookmark button—the so-called "bookmarklet"—at http://www.facebook.com/share_options.php.

If you follow the directions shown in Figure 5.10 and install the Facebook bookmarklet, you can click it while browsing. You can share the page you're currently viewing (whether or not it's on Facebook), as well as add a comment to that page.

The bookmarklet is of most use to Facebook members as they browse the Internet. It's of less use to marketers. However, another type of button is significant for marketers, as discussed next.

Posting Items from Partner Websites

Many websites that partner with Facebook display a Facebook share button. The middle of Figure 5.11 shows such a button. It's a stylized f for Facebook, on the *New York Times* website.

Figure 5.11

The Facebook button.

Clicking this button allows you to post the article you're viewing to your profile, as shown in Figure 5.12.

Figure 5.12

Posting a news article to Facebook.

As you can imagine, allowing Facebook members to post on Facebook—which adds the item to their friends' news feeds—gets the word out pretty quickly. It's a great marketing tool.

Deleting Posts

Sometimes you'll post an item and then wake up the next day and say, "What was I thinking?" For those items, it's good to know that you can delete posts.

To delete a post, click the Posted Items link on the left of any logged-in Facebook page (remembering that you might have to first click the "more" link to see the Posted Items link). Clicking the Posted Items link opens the posts page, as shown in Figure 5.13.

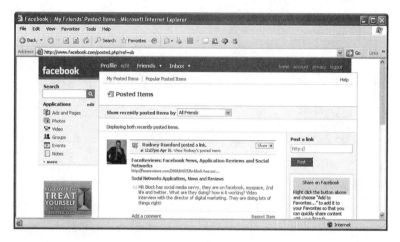

Figure 5.13
The posts page.

Click the My Posted Items tab near the top of Figure 5.13. This opens the page shown in Figure 5.14.

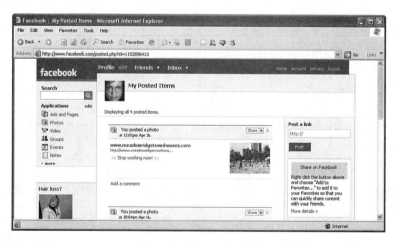

Figure 5.14
Taking a look at your posts.

Each of your posts is displayed on this page. You can delete the ones you want to remove by clicking the small X that appears in the upper right of the entry for each post. Facebook asks for confirmation, as shown in Figure 5.15.

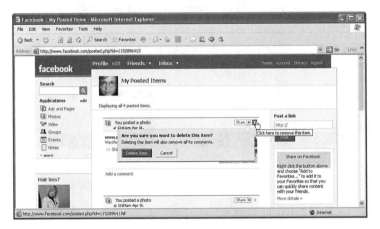

Figure 5.15
Deleting a posted item.

Clicking the Delete Item button deletes the item. Presto—there goes last night's mistake.

As you can see, posted items can give you free advertising. They appear in your friends' news feeds. Things grow virally on Facebook primarily through news feeds.

As mentioned, you must be careful not to spam this channel. At the bottom of Figure 5.13, you can see the Report Item link that your friends can use to report you as a spammer. And that's bad news.

Now we'll shift gears and talk about where you can spam in Facebook: ads. Every Facebook user is familiar with ads, because they appear at the lower left of just about every logged-in page. They can also appear in people's news feeds (which gives much better click-through rates).

We'll discuss them next.

What, in your experience, is the single most important topic or technique to know about Facebook marketing?

Facebook is all about viral marketing. If you can't calculate a v-factor, you'll never know if or when you're successful. You've got to be able to measure it otherwise you're throwing apps against a wall and seeing what sticks. Traditional marketing is irrelevant on Facebook because user acquisition costs are prohibitive and promotional channels are limited.

Mark Pincus, CEO, Zynga Game Network

Using Ads

Facebook introduced social ads in November 2007 to replace Facebook Flyers, and they've come to be accepted by Facebook members.

Facebook has two primary types of ads: standard ads and social ads.

There Are Ads, and Then There Are Social Ads

The first type of ad you see on Facebook is the normal type of click-through ad you see on the Internet. As shown on the left side of Figure 5.16, it's just an image with some text. When you click the ad, you are taken to a destination such as a Facebook page for the business or a site entirely off Facebook.

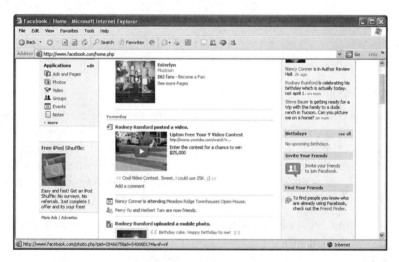

Figure 5.16
A Facebook ad.

It's most common for Facebook ads to take you offsite. But it's also worth noting that Facebook ads are probably the quickest way to grow an audience for your Facebook pages unless you want to take the time to build a big friends list.

The other kind of ad is a social ad. You can see an example in the center of Figure 5.17. It's a page in which Facebook explains the purpose of social ads—http://www.facebook.com/business/?socialads.

Figure 5.17
A Facebook social ad.

Here's how Facebook describes social ads:

> "Instead of creating an advertisement and hoping that it reaches the right customers, you can create a Facebook Social Ad and target it precisely to the audience you choose. The ads can also be shown to users whose friends have recently engaged with your Facebook Page or engaged with your website through Facebook Beacon. Social Ads are more likely to influence users when they appear next to a story about a friend's interaction with your business."

Facebook social ads allow your businesses to become part of people's daily conversations. Ads can be displayed in the ad space on the left, visible to users as they browse Facebook to connect with their friends. Ads also can appear in the context of a news feed, attached to relevant social stories. The social stories, such as a friend's becoming a fan of your Facebook page or a friend's taking an action on your website, make your ad more interesting and relevant. Social ads are placed in highly visible parts of the site without interrupting the user experience on Facebook.

In other words, social ads are ads that attempt to get into the social conversation. Facebook connects them by reading the text of news feed items, for example. If there's a connection with a social ad, Facebook puts the social ad in.

For example, in Figure 5.17 you can see the news feed text "Meagan Marks gave a 4-star rating to the movie Top Gun" in the social ad. The social ad that's been paired with it has the title "Blockbuster Total Access Online," which clearly matches up with the movie review.

Cost Per Click or Cost Per Thousand?

When you create an ad on Facebook, you can create it as a cost-per-click (CPC) or cost-per-thousand impressions (CPM) ad. (M is the Roman numeral for 1,000.)

Yes, you have to pay for ads on Facebook. If you're unwilling to pay for them, Facebook won't give you any ad space. CPC and CPM are the two payment options. Which one is right for you?

Use the CPC option if it's important to you that people click your ad and go to your link. For example, if you're advertising a Facebook page or a standard web page, using CPC is usually a good idea. You pay only when people click your ad and navigate to your web resource. The current minimum cost per click is $0.01.

On the other hand, it's better to use the CPM method if what's important to you is getting the word out about what you're advertising. For example, if your ad shows a banner for an opera, it might matter more to you that people see the banner than click the ad and go to a website.

Each "impression" of CPM means that your ad is displayed.

With CPM ads, you can also choose whether you want to have your ads appear on the left of Facebook pages (in the "ad space") or in news feeds. News feeds are more effective, but also more expensive. The current minimum CPM is $0.15 for the ad space and $0.15 for news feeds.

In addition, note that the minimum daily budget for both CPC and CPM is $5 per day. Also, your budget must be at least two times the CPC or CPM you have specified. For example, if you specify a $3 CPC, your daily budget must be at least $6.

When you create an ad, you specify the maximum you want to pay for each click or each one thousand impressions.

Bidding for Ad Presentation

When you create your ad, you can specify how much you want to bid for CPC or CPM. (That's one of the things you can change after you've created the ad. You can't change ad content. For that, you have to create a new ad.)

Facebook has many ads competing for the same space, so it chooses the one(s) that can pay the most. So if you've bid too low, your ad may never appear.

On the other hand, that doesn't mean you'll automatically be charged your maximum bid every time someone clicks your ad or it is displayed. Facebook increments the price you pay only until it's over the next contender ad and then charges you that.

For example, if the maximum bid of another ad is $0.25, and your maximum bid is $0.30, your ad is displayed, not the other ad. When that ad is clicked (CPC) or displayed (CPM), you aren't charged your maximum bid of $0.30. That's not to say Facebook will necessarily charge you $0.26, but the point is that Facebook doesn't automatically charge you your maximum bid every time. You'll see how you're being charged in the next chapter.

Now you're ready to create your first ad and put it in motion.

What insightful pieces of advice would you most want new marketers on Facebook to know?

Get going. Get an app built and test its virality. Don't let perfect be the enemy of good. Your users are the best product mangers you could ask for. They'll tell you what to build next and what's broken. Save the polish for v2.0!

Mark Pincus, CEO, Zynga Game Network

Creating an Ad

So what's the first step of creating your ad? Getting the creative juices flowing? Choosing a snappy image? Calling in the ad team to design irresistible ad copy?

Nope. The first step is to set up a Facebook account to let you pay for your ad.

Setting Up Your Account

To set up your account to pay for an ad (and anything else on Facebook, such as gifts), click the account link that appears in the upper right of all logged-in Facebook pages. This opens the account page shown in Figure 5.18.

Your name and email address are already entered.

Find the line for Credit Cards, and click the "manage" link on the right. In the page that appears, enter the cardholder's name, the card number, expiration date, and so on. Then click Save.

You've created a new account. Facebook can charge you now. Don't you feel secure?

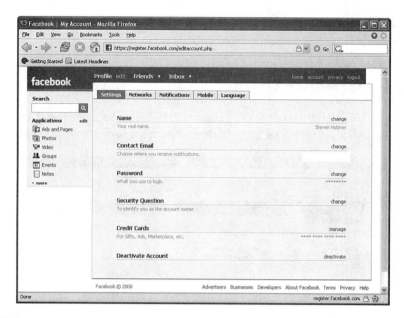

Figure 5.18
The account page.

Starting Your Ad

Starting an ad is simple. Facebook is pushing them, so you can find links to the process all over the place. The most prominent link is the Advertisers link at the bottom of every logged-in Facebook page. Clicking that link displays the page shown in Figure 5.19.

Figure 5.19
The Facebook Ads page.

This is the Facebook ads page (http://www.facebook.com/ads/). It pushes social ads and Facebook pages.

Choosing What to Advertise

To create a new ad, click the Get Started button or the Create Social Ad link at the bottom of the page (not visible in Figure 5.19). You are taken to the page shown in Figure 5.20.

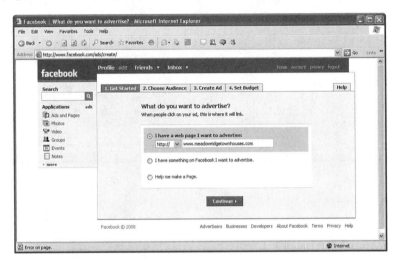

Figure 5.20
Creating a Facebook ad.

We'll create an ad to advertise a real estate development, Meadow Ridge Townhouses, at www.meadowridgetownhouses.com. You can see that URL entered in the "I have a web page I want to advertise" box in Figure 5.20.

You can also advertise Facebook events, groups, or pages by selecting the "I have something on Facebook I want to advertise" radio button, as shown in Figure 5.21.

Note that you can also make a new Facebook page by selecting the "Help me make a Page" radio button.

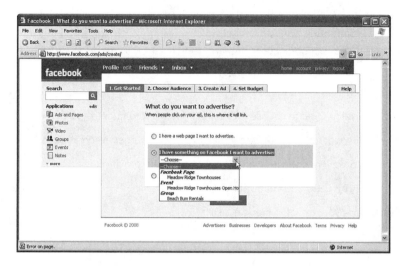

Figure 5.21
Selecting Facebook resource options.

Choosing Your Audience

Click the "I have a web page I want to advertise" radio button for Meadow Ridge
Townhouses. Clicking the Continue button displays the Choose Audience tab, shown in
Figure 5.22.

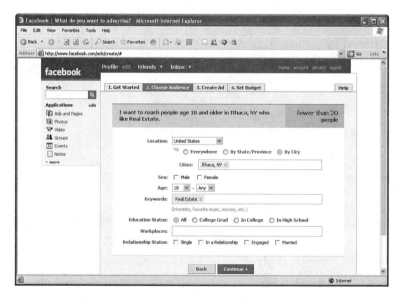

Figure 5.22
Choosing the audience for your ad.

This is one of the most powerful aspects of advertising on Facebook: the ability to target your audience with great precision. Facebook users innocently supply all this information when they create a Facebook account—and then it's used for targeted advertising. Pretty sneaky.

Here are the items on this page:

- Location: Allows you to choose the country you want to target, or all countries.
  - Everywhere: Lets you specify that you want to target everywhere in the country.
  - By State/Province: Lets you specify the state or province.
  - By City: Lets you select by city.
- Sex: Choose your target audience's sex.
  - Male
  - Female
- Age: Choose your target audience's age.
- Keywords: Select keywords, which have to match a list that Facebook displays.
- Education Status: Lets you choose your audience's education status.
  - All
  - College Grad
  - In College
  - In High School
- Workplaces: Lets you target by workplace.
- Relationship Status: Lets you target by relationship status—targeting singles, for example.
  - Single
  - In a Relationship
  - Engaged
  - Married

It's annoying from a marketer's point of view that you're not free to select any keyword, as you would with, say, Google's AdWords or Yahoo! marketing. You have to choose what Facebook offers. If your city isn't in the drop-down list that appears when you type the name of a city, for example, you're out of luck.

This is annoying, because the keywords are how Facebook makes your ad into a social ad. They are also how Facebook matches social discourse to your ad. For example, if you target a specific movie or event, your ad can show up when people see that movie or sign up to attend that event.

That's cool, but in practice, the keywords are very limited. And if you're over 30, be prepared to have never heard of most of the keywords, because they are targeted at the 20-something crowd.

Figure 5.23 shows keyword selection.

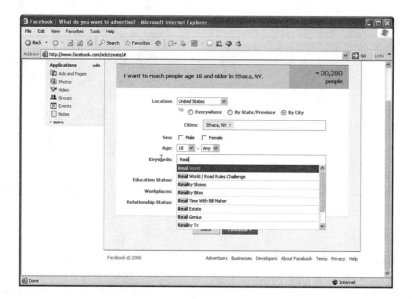

Figure 5.23
Choosing keywords.

If you're marketing something connected with current popular culture, you're all set. But if you're marketing apartments, you aren't likely (currently, anyway) to get many social ads. Your ads will appear as standard ads.

Creating the Ad

Clicking Continue in Figure 5.22 brings you to the Create Ad tab, as shown in Figure 5.24.

Here's what's on this page:

- Title: The title for your ad.

- Body: The text your ad displays.

- Photo: The photo you want displayed in your ad. Note that "Images will be resized to fit inside a 110px by 80px box. Use 3:4 or 16:9 aspect ratio for best results."

- Add Social Actions to my ad: This lets you choose the Facebook sources, such as a page or group that you're an admin of, that will generate social ads.

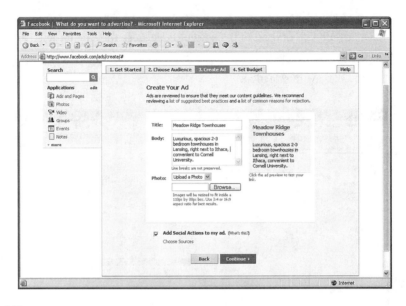

Figure 5.24
Creating your ad.

It can be worth taking a look at the Facebook ad guidelines at http://www.
facebook.com/ad_guidelines.php before proceeding. The following list summarizes
what's not allowed. (However, this is not a complete summation of the Ad Guidelines. For
the full story, see the URL just mentioned.)

- Accounts: No multiple accounts.

- Landing pages/destination URLs: Ads that contain a URL or domain in the body must
  link to that same URL or domain.

- Accurate ad text: Ad must not be misleading.

- Grammar, spelling, and capitalization: Ads must use correct spelling, text must make
  sense, and so on.

- Punctuation and symbols: Repeated and unnecessary punctuation or symbols are not
  allowed.

- Language and image content: "Ads may not contain, facilitate or promote adult content,
  including nudity, sexual terms and/or images of people in positions or activities that are
  excessively suggestive or sexual." "Ads may not contain, facilitate or promote offensive,
  profane, vulgar, obscene, or inappropriate language."

- Content restrictions: According to Facebook, the following are not allowed:

    - Liquor, beer, or wine

    - Tobacco products

- Ammunition or firearms
- Gambling, including, without limitation, any online casino, sports books, bingo, or poker
- Ringtones
- Software downloads, freeware, or shareware
- Scams, illegal activity and/or illegal contests, pyramid schemes, or chain letters
- Uncertified pharmaceutical products
- Adult friend finders or dating sites with a sexual emphasis
- Web cams or surveillance equipment
- Web-based nonaccredited colleges that offer degrees
- Inflammatory religious content
- Politically religious agendas and/or any known associations with hate, criminal, and/or terrorist activities
- Political content that exploits political agendas or uses "hot button" political issues for commercial use, regardless of whether the advertiser has a political agenda
- Hate speech, whether directed at an individual or group, whether based on the race, sex, creed, national origin, religious affiliation, marital status, sexual orientation, or language of the individual or group

- Facebook references: "Ads are not permitted to mention or refer to Facebook."
- No incentives: There is no incentive for clicking ads.
- Prices, discounts, and free offers: "If an ad includes a price, discount, or 'free' offer, the advertisement must clearly state what action or set of actions is required to qualify for the offer."
- Copyrights and trademarks: "Advertiser must have intellectual property rights to the creative and be permitted to display such creative as advertising on the Facebook Site."
- Spam: "No ad may contain, facilitate or promote 'spam' or other advertising or marketing content that violates applicable laws, regulations or industry standards."
- Downloads: "No ad is permitted to contain or link, whether directly or indirectly, to a site that contains software downloads, freeware, or shareware." "No ad is permitted to facilitate or promote (or contain a link to a site that facilitates or promotes)."

Also not allowed are viruses and spyware.

To upload a photo to your ad, click the Browse button and navigate to the photo. Figure 5.25 shows an uploaded photo for the ad.

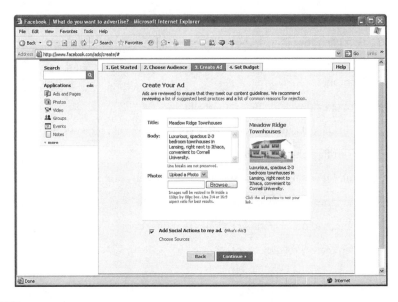

Figure 5.25
Uploading a photo for the ad.

Note that a preview of your ad appears on the right as you type and upload photos.

The "Add Social Actions to my ad" check box lets you specify the sources of social actions that Facebook tries to match your ad's keywords to. You can add any groups or pages you're an admin of, as shown at the bottom of Figure 5.26.

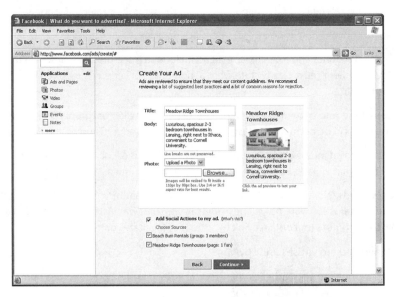

Figure 5.26
Making your ad a social ad.

In Figure 5.26 I've clicked the Choose Sources link, and Facebook lists the group and page that I'm an admin of.

That's how you tell Facebook what resources you want to watch for social actions that social ads can be tied to—by selecting them here.

Before leaving this page, it's important that you test the URL your ad is linked to. You can do that by clicking the ad preview or by right-clicking the ad preview and selecting Open Link in a New Window.

In this case, the link opens the Meadow Ridge Townhouses site, as shown in Figure 5.27. Cool.

Figure 5.27
The Meadow Ridge Townhouses page.

Setting the Budget for Your Ad

Clicking Continue brings you to the meat of the issue, from Facebook's point of view—how much you're willing to pay.

Figure 5.28 shows the Set Budget tab.

Figure 5.28
Budgeting a pay-per-click ad.

This tab has two subtabs—Pay for Clicks and Pay for Views.

The Pay for Clicks subtab is selected by default, as shown in Figure 5.28. Facebook starts you at a default budget of $25 a day. Adjust the budget to the amount you want to spend each day, bearing in mind that $5 is the minimum.

- Budget is the most you want to spend per day.

- Bid is how much you are willing to pay per click. Facebook often makes a suggestion here ("Suggested bid"), but it doesn't do that for our ad.

- Schedule lets you select when you want to start running your ad:

  - Run my ad continuously starting today

  - Run my ad only during specified dates: If you select this option, Facebook asks you for specific dates.

If you prefer paying per thousand views, click the Pay for Views subtab, which displays the page shown in Figure 5.29.

How much should you budget for your ad? In general, you should budget as little as you can to get the results you want. Bear in mind that comparing results to your advertising cost is a balancing act—don't go overboard to the point where advertising becomes unprofitable.

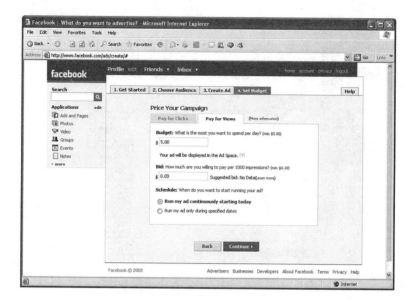

Figure 5.29
Budgeting a pay-per-view ad.

You can track your results using the Campaign Insights feature discussed in the next chapter. If you run multiple ads, you can track how they do compared to each other, and hone your campaign.

Particularly sensitive are the bids per click or per view. If your ad has a lot of competition, and if your competition is willing to pay more, your ad may never be shown. That's something you'll be able to track and rectify. Setting the daily maximum budget and the pay-per-click or pay-per-view bids are two of the few things you can change about an ad after it's been created.

Review Your Ad

When you click the Continue link shown in Figure 5.29, Facebook allows you to review your ad, as shown in Figure 5.30.

Looks good. Click the Place Order button on this page to start your ad.

Figure 5.30
Reviewing your ad.

Congratulations

Congratulations. You've just created your first ad, as shown in Figure 5.31.

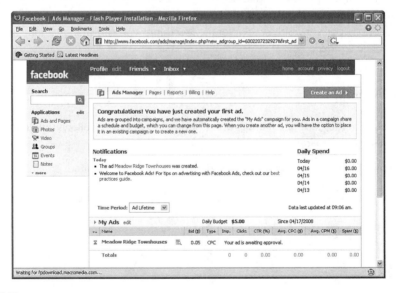

Figure 5.31
You just created your first ad.

You receive this email from Facebook:

Dear [Your Name]:

Welcome to Facebook Ads and congratulations on creating your first ad!

We wanted to let you know about some resources that will help you get the most out of your advertising experience.

Ad Manager:

View statistics, optimize your ad, or create a new campaign.

http://www.facebook.com/ads/manage/?act=[your account number]

Online Help:

Get answers to common questions.

http://www.facebook.com/help.php

Best Practices:

A compilation of tips to improve the quality of your ad.

http://www.facebook.com/ads/best_practices.php

Support:

Your direct line to our dedicated team of ad professionals.

http://www.facebook.com/cs_forms/fshelp.php

Please do not hesitate to reach out to the Facebook Ads support team with any questions or feedback on your experience. We look forward to working with you.

Sincerely,

The Facebook Ads Team

You might note the reference in this email to Facebook's list of best advertising practices, at http://www.facebook.com/ads/best_practices.php. Here are the topics covered in that list:

1. Identify your advertising goals
2. Targeting
3. Keyword targeting
4. Make your product stand out
5. Keep your ad simple
6. Use a strong call to action

7. Use an image

8. Landing pages

9. Keep the user experience in mind

10. Evaluate your campaign performance and make the necessary changes

You've created an ad and got it started. Now it's time to optimize and monitor its performance, which you'll do in the next chapter.

Optimizing and Monitoring Your Advertising

In this chapter:

Monitoring Facebook ads

Understanding ads

Getting ad metrics

Tuning and optimizing ads

Modifying ads

Now that your ad is created, you can watch its performance. Watching your ads' performance is a crucial part of advertising—you need to tune that performance to get the maximum bang for the buck. Because you've created an ad and a Facebook page, you see an Ads and Pages link on the left of every logged-in Facebook page. Clicking that link lets you manage your ads.

When you click the Ads and Pages link, the page shown in Figure 6.1 appears.

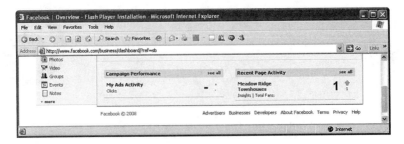

Figure 6.1
Your ad campaign.

You can manage your ads with the Campaign Performance section on this page. Clicking the "see all" link opens your campaign(s), as shown in Figure 6.2.

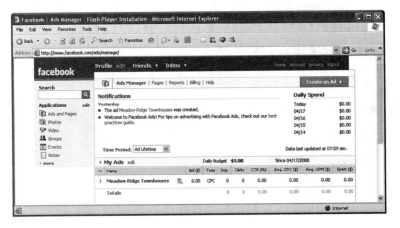

Figure 6.2
The details of your ad campaign in the Ads Manager.

Let's take a look at what is shown in this campaign.

Understanding Your Campaign

It's time now to understand what's going on with your campaign. First, note the Time Period drop-down list box shown in Figure 6.2. It allows you to select the period for which you want to see your campaign's performance. Here are the options:

- Ad Lifetime
- Last 24 hours
- Last 7 days

Selecting from these options lets you choose a time window during which you want to see how your ad performed.

The page tells you when the data displayed was last updated: "Data last updated at 07:59 am." Note that your campaign's data always has a delay before it's displayed.

The next line, My Ads, gives you a little data about your overall ads—in particular, your daily budget and the date you started your campaign. Note that your daily budget is one of the few items you can change. (In this respect, Facebook ads are much more limited than Google or Yahoo! ads. There aren't many ways to tune them.)

Each ad you run in the campaign has a line of info, as shown in Figure 6.2. Here are the items you see for every ad:

- Name: The name of the ad.
- Bid ($): The amount you're bidding, for either CPC or CPM (see Chapter 5).
- Type: CPC or CPM. Currently, these are the only two types of ads Facebook offers.
- Imp.: The number of impressions so far—that is, the number of times your ad has been displayed.
- Clicks: How many times Facebook members have clicked your ad.
- CTR (%): The click-through ratio—that is, your ad's percentage of the total impressions that are clicked.
- Avg. CPC ($): The average cost per click. Facebook doesn't automatically charge you.
- Avg. CPM ($): The average cost per thousand impressions.
- Spent ($): The amount you've spent for the time period you've selected on the ad.

This kind of information can help you tune and optimize your ad, as discussed in the next few sections.

Tuning the Number of Impressions

The number of impressions is how many times your ad's been visible. It isn't just how many times Facebook has had the opportunity to display your ad; it's how many times Facebook has chosen to display your ad.

Bear in mind that your ad isn't automatically displayed if it's competing for space with other ads. If the other ads outbid you, yours doesn't show up.

So if the number of impressions is low, or zero, consider upping the amount you bid for the ad (you'll see how to do that in a few pages). In fact, Facebook often cheerfully suggests a big increase in the amount you bid. Ignore it. (As you'll see, Facebook happily suggests that I increase my ad's bid from $0.05 to $0.42, or about 50% higher than an ad I run on Google that gets about 1.5 million impressions a day.) If you're not getting any impressions, increment the ad's bid, but don't go overboard. Increment it just enough to make sense for you.

Keep in mind that the real criterion for success of an ad campaign is sales, not impressions.

Tuning the Click-Through Ratio

The click-through ratio (CTR) is more under your control than Facebook's. Facebook's job is to display your ad, and your ad's job is to pull in prospects.

If your click-through ratio is too small, consider whether you've targeted your ad correctly. You have to create a new ad if you want to change the targeting, so the best idea is to create a new ad and run it and your current ad and compare CTRs.

That's the way to see at a glance which ad is pulling in prospects—comparing ad performance. It doesn't cost anything to create a new ad (although running it might be a different story). So consider creating and running at least three ads at the same time to tune the best one for you.

What's a CTR that's too low? It depends on a lot of factors. For example, you might have no choice but to run an ad for a large, nontargeted population, and you end up with a low CTR. But anything with a CTR less than 0.01% should raise a red flag.

Tuning the Average CPC

For cost-per-click (CPC) ads, you should watch the average cost per click carefully. As mentioned, Facebook does not automatically charge you your maximum bid every time someone clicks your ad or displays it a thousand times. You're actually charged based on what your nearest competitor is offering.

In fact, to give you ad space, Facebook increments the amount it charges you by just a little over the runner-up ad for the same space. So watch the CPC. If you're bidding too high, the CPC will be low compared to your bid.

If you're bidding too low, Facebook will be sure to tell you, as you're about to see.

What insightful pieces of advice would you most want new marketers on Facebook to know?

Facebook is a social media platform, like an "Online Cocktail Party" if I may share an analogy, where friends and acquaintances can connect and gather to keep up with each other, share photos, links, and videos, and learn more about the people they meet.

You could barge in to this "cocktail party" with guns blazing, pitching what you have to offer. This is a surefire way to get kicked out of the party. Don't do this.

The proper etiquette at a cocktail party is to "put on your party hat," be professional yet friendly, listen to understand the vibe of discussions, join in conversations, and add value where you can build likeability, trust, and respect. Only then do you have buy-in to attract your new connections to what you have to offer, not before.

Sherman Hu, creator and producer, WordpressTutorials.com

Getting an Ad's Daily Details

What you see in Figure 6.2 is only an overview of your ads. You can also get more daily details on each ad by clicking its name in the table shown in Figure 6.2, which opens the page shown in Figure 6.3.

The first thing you notice when you look at the current ad's details is that Facebook is urgently suggesting that I increase the ad's bid to start getting impressions.

Here's the message from Facebook: "The bid on your ad may be too low to receive a significant amount of impressions. We recommend raising your bid to at least $0.42."

Actually, $0.42 strikes me as too much for the type of ad we've created. How much you spend on CPC is up to your expected return per clicker. For the ad we've created, I'd increase the CPC to $0.20, and then $0.25, and so on. But if the cost per click becomes too great for the expected return per clicker, I'd question if my ad is worth running. (The Meadow Ridge Townhouses website gets a couple thousand clicks per month, from which two to four people become actual renters, so all that has to be budgeted in.)

So the correct setting for CPC depends on the expected return per clicker. For a site that relies on Google's AdSense ads to make any revenue (such as a site that offers thousands of menus and displays "Ad by Google" in the margins), the CPC must be very low, on the order of the minimum possible—$0.05 or so. Otherwise, it doesn't make sense to run the ad. On the other hand, for ads that sell mortgages, each click could be worth $1 or $2.

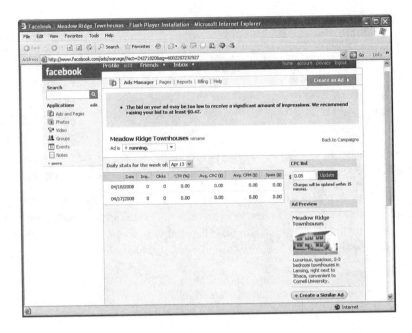

Figure 6.3
An ad's daily details.

Note the table shown in Figure 6.3:

Date	Imp.	Clicks	CTR (%)	Avg. CPC ($)	Avg. CPM ($)	Spent ($)
04/18/2008	0	0	0.00	0.00	0.00	0.00
04/17/2008	0	0	0.00	0.00	0.00	0.00

This table shows you your ad's daily performance, which can be useful information. For example, at Meadow Ridge Townhouses, we used to get almost no calls on the weekend, but we noticed that the number of hits was steady, even on the weekend. We finally realized that lots of people thought rental companies are closed on the weekend—which also explained why we got a spike of calls on Monday. So we changed the site to invite people to call seven days a week, and this has evened out our traffic.

OK, so you've been tuning your ads. Now what can you actually change about a Facebook ad?

Changing Your Ad's Settings

You actually can change very little about an ad after you've created it, unlike other online advertising channels such as Google.

Here's Facebook's word on the subject:

> "Once your ad has been created, you can only change the cost per click or CPM for your ad. If you wish to change the targeting or content of your ad you will need to pause the ad and create a new one with the correct criteria. You can also use the 'Create a Similar Ad' function beneath any of your ads in the Ad Manager to recreate an ad and easily make changes to it."

It turns out that you can change the bid, your budget, and one or two other items, as discussed next.

Changing Your Bid

Take a look at the CPC Bid box shown in Figure 6.3. That's how you can change your bid for this ad.

Want to increase your bid for the whole ad? Just enter the new bid, and you're set.

Presumably, at some point, Facebook will be more sophisticated about this, allowing you to bid separately on different keywords. Some popular keywords are used by many advertisers, and Facebook might make them more expensive, while lowering the bid on less-popular words.

Changing Your Budget

You can also change the daily budget of your whole ad campaign. To do that, click the Ads and Pages link on the left, and then click the "see all" link in the ads section of the page. This brings up the Ads Manager, shown in Figure 6.2.

Next, click the "edit" link next to the My Ads title, opening the dialog box shown in Figure 6.4.

Here's where you can change your daily budget—the maximum amount you're willing to pay each day. You can set your daily budget as high as you want, as long as it doesn't surpass your spending limit, as discussed later.

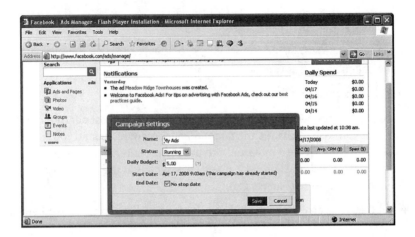

Figure 6.4
Setting your budget.

Pausing or Deleting Your Ad

Figure 6.3 shows the "Ad is" drop-down list box. Figure 6.4 shows the Status drop-down list box. Both these list boxes let you pause or delete your ad as needed.

Here are the choices in the list boxes:

- Running
- Paused
- Delete

As you can imagine, the Running option sets the ad to run, Paused pauses it, and Delete lets you delete the ad.

Modifying Your Ad

So what about modifying your ad? The news here is that, except for the items just discussed, you can't really modify an ad after you've launched it.

That means that you have to create a new ad. Fortunately, Facebook makes it relatively easy to create a new ad based on a current ad, which makes it easy to modify your current ad and run it as a new ad.

To create a new ad based on a current ad, open that ad in the Ads Manager by clicking the ad's title, opening the ad detail page shown in Figure 6.5.

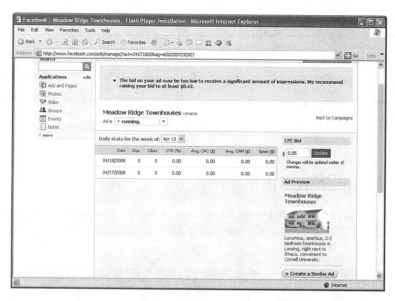

Figure 6.5
The Create a Similar Ad button.

Note the Create a Similar Ad button at the bottom right of Figure 6.5. Clicking that button opens the current ad as sort of a template, as shown in Figure 6.6.

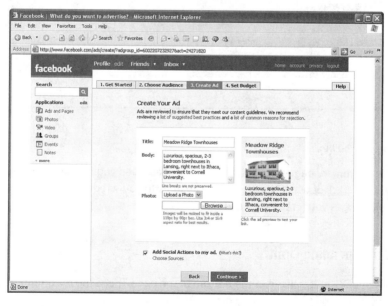

Figure 6.6
Creating a similar ad.

As shown in the figure, the pages and tabs that appear when you're creating a similar ad are the same pages you used when you created the ad in the first place.

In other words, effectively modifying an ad on Facebook isn't too difficult if you're willing to put up with creating a similar ad (with a different name to keep the two ads separate).

There's one more concept you have to master here—the daily spending limit. That's a different number from the ad bid and the daily budget.

Checking Your Billing

To see what you've been billed so far, you can check your Facebook advertising billing. Open an ad, as shown in Figure 6.3, and click the Billing tab. You see the page shown in Figure 6.7.

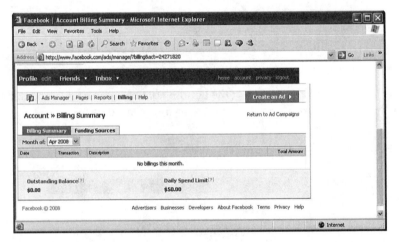

Figure 6.7
Checking your billing.

The Billing Summary page shows what Facebook has billed you for your campaign. Here you can keep track of what's going on with charges to your credit card. By default Facebook charges your credit card daily.

Your Daily Spending Limit

The Daily Spend Limit is listed at the bottom of the page. This is the maximum that Facebook allows you to spend every day.

The daily budget is the amount you designate to spend as a maximum. The ad bid price is the amount you'll bid for that ad. The daily spending limit is different—it's the amount that Facebook is willing to let you spend, maximum. Here's what Facebook says about it:

> "Your Daily Spend Limit works like a credit limit on a credit card. This is separate from the Daily Budgets that you set for each of your campaigns. The Daily Spend Limit represents the most that our system will ever allow you to spend in one day. If the combined Daily Budgets of all your campaigns is less than your current Daily Spend Limit, you will never hit your Daily Spend Limit. Our system will never charge you more than the total of the Daily Budgets that you have set for your active campaigns."

Clearly, $50 a day won't cut it for the big firms—or even many of the smaller ones. So what does Facebook have to say about increasing your daily spending limit?

> "The Daily Spend Limit for your account is predetermined by our system when you open your account. Our system will periodically increase your Daily Spend Limit based on a history of successful payments on your account."

Well, fine, but many people have advertising needs that are bigger than what Facebook decides to give them. If that includes you, contact Facebook at http://www.facebook.com/cs_forms/fshelp.php.

Integrated Solutions

If your annual budget is $50,000 or more, the picture changes, however. In that case, Facebook has entire teams to take over and handle your advertising. Just go to http://www.facebook.com/business/contact.php, as shown in Figure 6.8, and enter a budget of $50,000 or so.

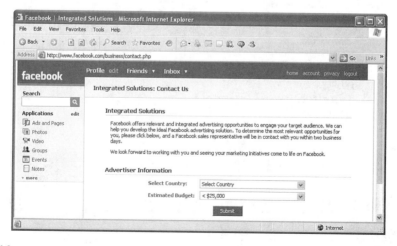

Figure 6.8
The Integrated Solutions page.

Trust me—you'll get a call. As the text on this page says:

> "Facebook offers relevant and integrated advertising opportunities to engage your target audience. We can help you develop the ideal Facebook advertising solution. To determine the most relevant opportunities for you, please click below, and a Facebook sales representative will be in contact with you within two business days.

> "We look forward to working with you and seeing your marketing initiatives come to life on Facebook."

Have you made any mistakes—what should new marketers avoid?

Always comply with Facebook rules, they do not play around with their rules—we made a few mistakes when we started out and definitely paid a price for that.

Sunmit Singh, CEO, RootsGear, Inc., www.rootsgear.com

Exporting Your Campaign's Performance

You can also export your marketing reports, such as CPC, CTR, and so on, into the Excel (.xls) or comma-separated values (.csv) format, which is a common generic format for such data reports.

To export your advertising summary to a report, click the Reports tab in the Ads Manager, opening the page shown in Figure 6.9.

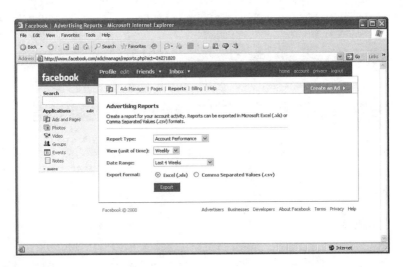

Figure 6.9
Exporting reports.

The first item you can select on this page is the type of report you want to generate. Here are the possibilities:

- Account Performance
- Campaign Performance
- Ad Performance

You also can select the reports by time period in the View box, which lists these options:

- Monthly
- Weekly
- Daily

You can specify the date range you want to include in your report in a limited number of ways. Here are the possibilities for the Date Range box:

- Yesterday
- Last Week
- Last Two Weeks
- Last 30 Days
- This Week (since Sunday)
- Last 4 Weeks
- Last 12 Weeks
- Last 24 Weeks
- This Month (since the 1st)
- Last 3 months
- Last 6 months
- Last 12 months

Finally, you choose the export format:

- Excel (.xls)
- Comma-separated values (.csv)

After making your selections, click the Export button, and you're done. Nice.

Using Campaign Insights for Pages

Besides getting statistics for ads, you can also get statistics for pages—that is, how many people have been visiting your page(s).

You do that through the Insights link that you find in the Ads and Pages Manager (or the Pages Manager if you don't have any ads). Just click Ads and Pages on the left of any logged-in Facebook page (or Pages if you don't have any ads). This opens the page shown in Figure 6.10.

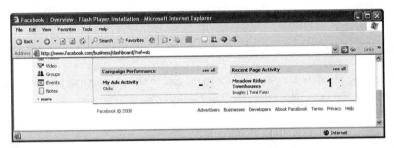

Figure 6.10
The campaign insights link.

Note the Insights link near the lower right of Figure 6.10. Clicking it brings up the page shown in Figure 6.11.

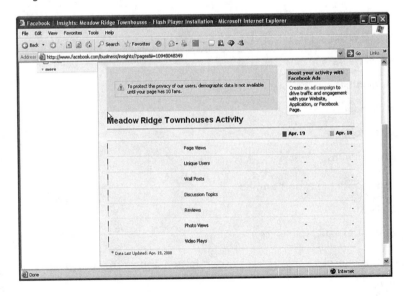

Figure 6.11
The insights page for Facebook pages.

Note the items listed on this page. You have page views, unique users, Wall posts, and more. We'll go through these briefly here. Note that the page we developed hasn't had any activity lately. If it had, you'd see a histogram at the bottom of this page, showing the numbers graphically in a bar chart.

Page Views

This is the number of hits your page has gotten, which clearly is an important indication of how many Facebook members have been coming to your page.

Unique Users

This section lists how many people have come to your page. Knowing the total page views is good, but if you have a very active community, you might be seeing the same people over and over.

The Unique Users item tells you how many separate people have been coming to your page. Taken together with the Page Views, you can get an idea of the average number of page views per unique user. This is a good indication of how involved your users are with your page.

Wall Posts

The Wall Posts section also indicates how involved people are with your site. This section lets you know at a glance how active your Wall has been (and, of course, that could be a good thing or a bad thing).

To tune the various parts of your page, this is one of the statistics that bears watching.

Discussion Topics

This is another measure of how interested users are in your site. The discussion section of a page is there to let users start and respond to discussion threads.

If your users are involved with your brand and you're generating a lot of buzz, you'll see it in this section.

Reviews

Users also can post reviews of your brand, product, event, and so on on your page. You can monitor the number of reviews posted at a glance with this statistic.

Like discussion topics or posts, however, you have to note that reviews can be positive or negative. If you're getting reviews, make sure that you read them to stay on top of things.

Photo Views

If you've uploaded images of your products or brands, you might be interested to learn how many people have been taking a look. Facebook tells you that in this section.

Photo views are a good indication of user interest in what you have to offer. To engage users, make sure you upload some flashy photos frequently, along with changing your page's content.

Video Plays

The same goes for videos. If you've uploaded any to your page, you can check this metric to see how many people have been watching them. This is a good way to stay in touch with your users and what's going on with your page.

Optimizing for Your Target Audience

In many ways, the advertising support on Facebook isn't as sophisticated as what you'll find in the various search engines such as Google and Yahoo!. Facebook makes up for that by letting you target your demographics with great precision, especially if you want to advertise for a particular location or college.

This precision is one of the main reasons to advertise on Facebook. Within its limitations, Facebook knows a heck of a lot more about, and can deliver, specific audiences far better than Google or Yahoo!.

We'll look at some aspects of targeting your audience next.

Determining Your Target Audience Size

When creating an ad, you can see the estimated target audience size for your selection criteria in the Choose Audience tab, as shown in Figure 6.12.

As shown in Figure 6.12, Facebook estimates 30,300 Facebook members in Ithaca, New York, who are between 18 and 65.

Figure 6.12
Determining your audience size.

Not bad, but let's see how that target audience changes if you target only male college students. Figure 6.13 shows the results: we're down to 8,400 members.

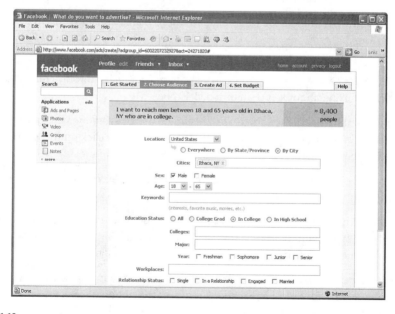

Figure 6.13
Narrowing your target audience.

Let's see how many of them have listed movies as a keyword that especially interests them (try to catch that, Google!). Figure 6.14 shows the results.

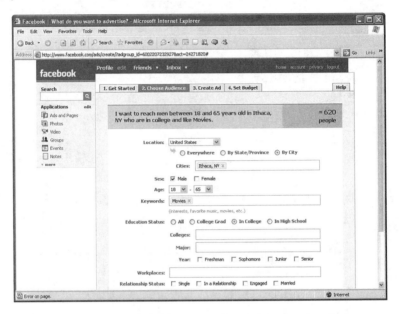

Figure 6.14
Narrowing your target audience still further.

We're down to an estimated 640 people (out of more than 40 million registered Facebook users).

That audience may be too small to get any results with your ad, however. Yes, the ad will be served to your audience when they're online, but if your click-through ratio is only 0.05%, you're talking about less than one click expected.

To expand our target audience again, we'll assume that not everyone who goes to see movies listed "movies" as one of their keywords. So remove (by clicking the X next to it) the criterion that the members must have listed movies as an interest.

We'll also limit our search to students at Cornell University, which is in Ithaca. Figure 6.15 shows the results.

As shown in Figure 6.15, this gives us an estimated target audience of 6,060 members to work with. That still might not be enough if you have a really small click-through ratio. There's one way to find out: give your ad a try, and see how it flies.

Note that although you can target cities and towns, Facebook is still growing in this area. If you select Austria, for example, Facebook removes the option of selecting which city or town in Austria you can target.

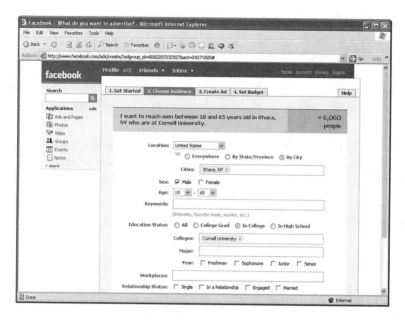

Figure 6.15
Narrowing your target audience even more.

How does Facebook narrow the search by geographic region? It does so by checking the user's IP address. This is great for colleges, but it might not be so useful if you're just looking for users in a small town, and the nearest cable operator that most people are connected to has its headquarters in a big city 60 miles away. For that reason, you might have a little trouble if you're targeting small cities or towns. You'd think Facebook could use the data that users give about their location when they sign up, but it doesn't.

Selecting Keywords

As you saw in the previous example, although selecting keywords sounds like a great way to identify users, in practice it can be too limiting unless you have a nationwide audience.

Some Facebook Ad Facts

Here are some facts about Facebook ads: the title of a Facebook ad is limited to 25 characters, and the body is limited to 135 characters.

Images should be no larger than 110 pixels by 80 pixels. If images are larger than that, Facebook resizes them. To avoid scrunched images, you may want to do the resizing yourself.

Currently you can pay for ads only with a credit card; Facebook accepts only Visa, MasterCard, and American Express. In general, your card is charged "once per Facebook billable day." However, Facebook reserves the right to charge you as often as every day, or as seldom as every few days. According to Facebook's documentation, it won't charge you more than once a day. This is just as well, because some card-issuing banks freeze your card if they see that kind of practice, which can be a sign of fraud or illegal use of the card.

The metrics on your ad can take a few hours to update, so if it doesn't seem that you're getting any clicks, wait a while and then check again. If you pause or stop an ad, it pauses or stops in an hour—at least, that's under "normal circumstances," according to Facebook.

Here's a question: can a Facebook ad target two or more distinct geographic regions? The answer: nope.

Onsite or Offsite Landing Pages

A big question for Facebook advertisers has been whether to send people to a Facebook page or an offsite, non-Facebook web page. Many veteran Facebook advertisers will tell you that you should always send people who click your ads to a Facebook page.

They say that because, for them, the benefits of a page outweigh the problems. Visitors to your page can become fans of the page, which is good for building a following. They can chat among themselves and build recognition of your brand. They can post discussions and share your page with their friends.

In other words, they can give you great public exposure.

That's all well and good if your goal is to build community and create a presence for your ad. But that's not the case with all ads.

Sometimes you just want to sell something. You want prospective customers to buy something right then and there, when they get to your site. And there's no way to set up Facebook pages to let you do that. For that, you need an offsite website.

So the onsite-versus-offsite debate comes down to your advertising goals. Are you trying to build community around your brand? Or are you trying to make a sale? If the latter, go with offsite landing pages.

Using the Marketplace

In this chapter:

- Welcome to the Marketplace
- Understanding Marketplace categories
- Navigating the Marketplace
- Listing an item
- Knowing the rules

Introducing the Marketplace

The Facebook Marketplace lets you buy and sell items, much like other classified ad-posting sites such as craigslist. Listing and buying on the Marketplace is easy. If you're selling individual items, this can be a great source of revenue.

The Facebook Marketplace is localized by region or network. That means, as with craigslist, you can browse items for sale or want ads in your local area. But you can also browse other regions by entering a city or state. You can't browse networks that you're not a member of.

When it comes to listing, you can post items to multiple networks, but you have to pay $1 per network per listing. Note that spamming is forbidden in the Marketplace, as it is throughout Facebook. Spam the Marketplace, and your account will be deleted.

It's my experience that the Marketplace doesn't have as many users as the more social aspects of Facebook, such as pages and profiles. Craigslist is better if you want to sell something. But if you've already listed on craigslist, the Marketplace is your next step.

The Marketplace has one advantage over craigslist. Responses on craigslist can be anonymous, but not with the Marketplace. When someone replies to your listing, you get access to his profiles—whether or not he's a friend.

Taking a Look at the Marketplace

Let's take a look at the Marketplace. You can reach it from any logged-in page by clicking the Marketplace link on the left (you may have to click the "more" link first). Figure 7.1 shows the Marketplace for my local network, Ithaca, NY.

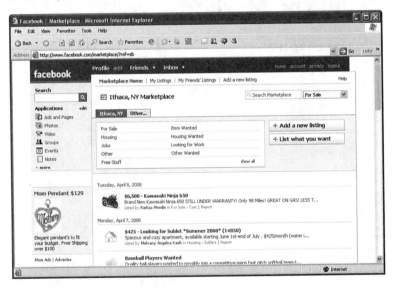

Figure 7.1
The Marketplace.

Let's see what's going on here.

Marketplace Categories

My local network's Marketplace is shown in Figure 7.1. Note the category links—For Sale, Item Wanted, and so on. These links come in pairs—selling and buying are complementary listings.

Here are the categories and what's in them—which is pretty obvious for the most part, starting with items that are for sale or wanted:

- For Sale

- Item Wanted

There's also a section for housing. This is where Meadow Ridge Townhouses goes:

- Housing

- Housing Wanted

There's a section for jobs, both offering and looking:

- Jobs

- Looking for Work

Unlike a fully detailed site like craigslist, that's about it. There are also two categories for everything else:

- Other

- Other Wanted

And there's a category for free items:

- Free Stuff

Like craigslist, the Marketplace is all about listing online classified ads with images, but it's a lot less developed than craigslist. You get the feeling that if Facebook made the site more central and gave the impression that it supported it more—for example, with 60 categories—it would attract more business.

Looking at a Category

If you click the For Sale link in Figure 7.1, the corresponding page appears, as shown in Figure 7.2.

As you can see, you can search the listings, which we'll get to in a moment. As you can also see, some featured listings are already available at the bottom of the page.

Figure 7.2
The For Sale items.

Looking at an Ad

Let's look at a specific ad. If you click the first item for sale in Figure 7.2, the $6,500 Kawasaki Ninja 650, a window pops up with the complete ad, as shown in Figure 7.3.

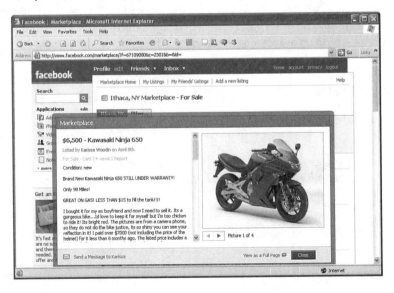

Figure 7.3
A Marketplace ad.

Note that the ad has an image, which is essential for selling in the Marketplace. Actually, this ad has four images, as indicated by the navigation arrows under the image and the text "Picture 1 of 4."

Note that the text is descriptive. There's a title in a large font, followed by the Facebook name of the poster and the ad's text.

What if you want to get in touch with the poster to make an offer? Just click the Send a Message to link at the lower left. When you do, the window expands as shown in Figure 7.4. You enter a subject and your message, type the words Facebook displays in an image, and click Send.

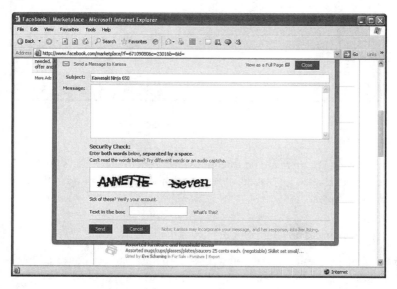

Figure 7.4
Sending a message about an ad.

That covers the Marketplace basics. Next you'll see how to search for the items you want.

Searching for Items

In the For Sale category shown in Figure 7.2, you can see links to the available subcategories: Books, Furniture, Tickets, Electronics, Cars, and Other. Besides displaying pages for these subcategories by clicking the links, you can search them using the Search box.

Say you want to search for an apartment in Ithaca, NY. Not just an apartment, but a townhouse. Go to the home page of the Marketplace (click the Marketplace Home link at the top of any Marketplace page) and click the Housing link. In the Housing page that opens, as shown in Figure 7.5, select Rentals/Apartments in the drop-down list box, type "townhouse" in the search box, and click Search.

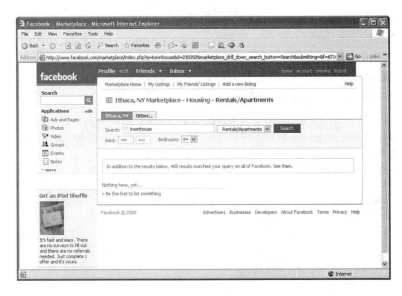

Figure 7.5
Searching for townhouses.

As shown in Figure 7.5, there are no townhouses for rent in my region's Marketplace yet. This is the perfect chance for Meadow Ridge Townhouses to get an ad in there, and we'll do that in a few pages.

Any advice on branding your company on Facebook?

Keep it simple and informal, sometimes the corporate branding turns people away especially if your target market is anywhere from 16–25 year olds.

Sunmit Singh, CEO of RootsGear, Inc., www.rootsgear.com

Browsing Other Regions and Networks

You might find it interesting that when Facebook couldn't find any townhouses in Ithaca, NY, it displays a link saying, "In addition to the results below, 485 results matched your query on all of Facebook. See them." Clicking that link displays townhouses for rent around the country, as shown in Figure 7.6.

A national search for townhouses might not be too useful if you're planning to live in Ithaca, NY, but what if you want to buy a VHS-to-DVD recorder? Or a book on French monasteries? Items like that can be shipped to you, so although you might start by searching in one geographic region, Facebook also notifies you of global results—something that craigslist doesn't do.

Figure 7.6
Finding townhouses.

You can join other networks in Facebook to search other areas, of course. Click the "account" link at the top right of any logged-in Facebook page, and then click the Networks tab. This opens the page shown in Figure 7.7.

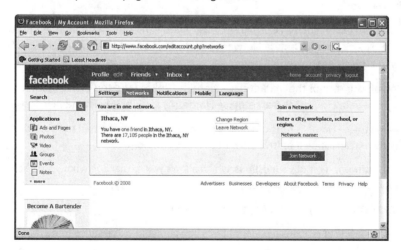

Figure 7.7
Joining networks.

When you join other networks, there are restrictions. You can't join (or browse) a college or workplace network unless you have an email address corresponding to the college or workplace's domain, for example.

But you don't need to belong to many networks to be able to browse their Marketplaces. So how do you browse the Marketplace outside your own networks? Click the Other tab shown in Figure 7.6, opening the browse window shown in Figure 7.8.

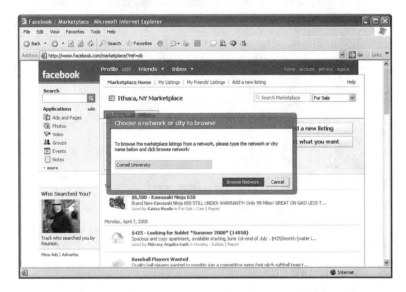

Figure 7.8
Browsing networks.

To browse a network, such as Cornell University, you can enter that name, as shown in Figure 7.8. Then click the Browse Network button. This opens the Cornell University network Marketplace, as shown in Figure 7.9.

To round off our tour of the Marketplace, note the links at the top of the Marketplace page, as shown in Figure 7.9: Marketplace Home, My Listings, My Friends' Listings:

- Marketplace Home is the home page for the Marketplace, opened to your primary network. Tabs appear for the other networks you belong to.

- My Listings is a list of your listings, which allows you to manage what you're selling or looking for in the Marketplace.

- My Friends' Listings is a list of your friend's listings.

- Add a new listing opens a page that lets you add your own listings to the Marketplace.

Examine the Add a new listing link in particular. It opens a new page that lets you create a classified ad in the Marketplace. You'll see how to do that next.

Figure 7.9
Browsing the Cornell University network.

Creating a Listing

It's time to create a listing on the Marketplace. Before we start, we want to note that there's quite a list of prohibited items that you can't post.

Listing an Item for Sale

So how do you create and place your own ad in the Facebook Marketplace? It's easy. Start at the Marketplace Home, as shown in Figure 7.10. You get there by clicking the Marketplace link on the left of any logged-in Facebook page (always recalling that you might have to click the "more" link to see the Marketplace link).

Click the Add a new listing button or the Add a new listing link in the upper right to go to the page shown in Figure 7.11.

Figure 7.10
The Marketplace home.

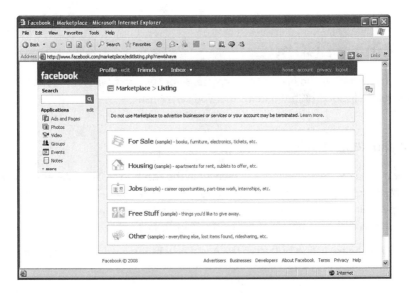

Figure 7.11
Creating a new listing.

Note the warning at the top of Figure 7.11: "Do not use Marketplace to advertise businesses or services or your account may be terminated." Clicking the "learn more" link displays this text:

"Do not post a listing in Marketplace if the listing is:

"Spam - the community believes the lister should buy an ad instead, examples:

"OK to list item details and provide a link to another listing site for more information

"NOT OK to advertise links to commercial websites (e.g. http://myfriendsnewcompany.com)

"NOT OK for the listing to simply link to another site

"NOT OK to list pyramid or promotional schemes (e.g. freeipods.com)

"NOT OK to post items too frequently

"Miscategorized - the community believes the listing is inappropriate for the category, examples:

"NOT OK to list items that are free in the for sale category

"NOT OK to list items in multiple categories

"Prohibited - the listing content violates the Marketplace Guidelines, examples:

"NOT OK to list firearms

"NOT OK to list fraudulent items"

You get the idea. Facebook is very protective of the Marketplace and its users. Note in particular that you can't post a link to a commercial website on the Marketplace.

Click the Housing link shown in Figure 7.11 to open the page shown in Figure 7.12.

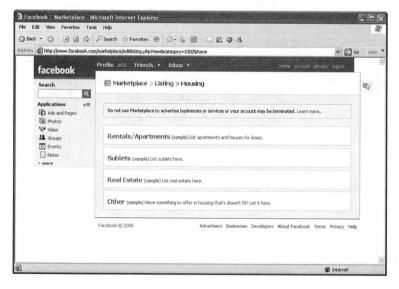

Figure 7.12
Creating a new housing listing.

These are the choices:

- Rentals/Apartments
- Sublets
- Real Estate
- Other: If you have something to offer in housing that doesn't fit in the other categories, you can list it here.

In this case, we're listing a rental, so click Rentals/Apartments. You see the page shown in Figures 7.13 and 7.14.

Here are the items to fill out when listing a rental:

- Title: The ad's title.
- Description: The description of the rental.
- Bedrooms: Maximum of eight allowed.
- Bathrooms: Maximum of eight allowed.
- Rent: List the rent here. You can specify these currencies:
  - U.S. dollars
  - Canadian dollars
  - Pounds sterling
  - Euros
- Street: The address of your rental.
- Cross Street: The cross street nearest your rental.
- Postal Code: The postal code of the rental. Many rental sites make the mistake of listing rentals only by zip code. This can be a problem if your rental is in a suburb of the main city that new renters don't know the zip code of. Facebook avoids that by listing rentals by network.
- Square Footage: The size of the rental in square feet.
- Allowed: Will you allow these items?:
  - Dogs
  - Cats
  - Smokers
- Profile: Select the "Add this listing to my profile" check box to add the listing to your profile.

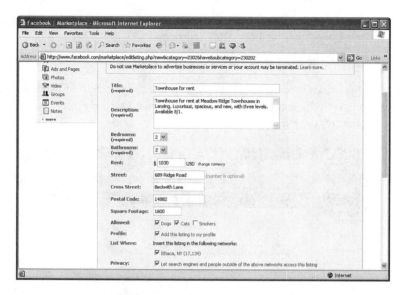

Figure 7.13
Creating a new rental listing, top half.

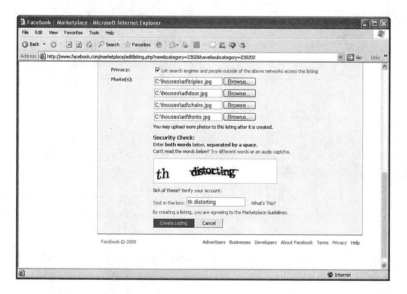

Figure 7.14
Creating a new rental listing, bottom half.

- List Where: What networks to list the listing in. In this case, we'll use this network:

    - Ithaca, NY (17,134)

- Privacy: If you want people outside the network to see the ad, select the "Let search engines and people outside of the above networks access this listing" check box.

- Photo(s): You're allowed four photos maximum. As the text says here, however, "You may upload more photos to this listing after it is created."

- Security Check: The usual Facebook check to make sure you're not an automated robot.

Click the Create Listing button to create the listing. You can see the new listing on the next page, along with the text "Your listing has been created. It will appear in the Marketplace shortly." (see Figure 7.15).

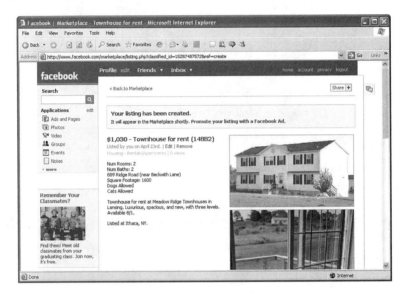

Figure 7.15
Your new listing has been created.

Please let us in on your vision for Facebook marketing in the future—any grand plans? Where is Facebook marketing heading?

Facebook marketing is at its peak right now. This will continue to benefit both the advertiser and consumer by giving the consumer more choices and the advertiser a wide range of demographics to choose from.

Only the skilled and experienced marketer will survive and be successful on Facebook. It is fairly easy to tell the difference between a new versus experienced marketer.

Sunmit Singh, CEO of RootsGear, Inc., www.rootsgear.com

Managing Your Listing

Want to see your new listing? Go to the Marketplace home and click the My Listings tab, as shown in Figure 7.16.

Figure 7.16
Your new listing.

Figure 7.16 shows the new ad as it will appear to people browsing the Marketplace. If you want to see your ad full size, as shown in Figure 7.17, click the title or photo.

Figure 7.17
Your new listing, full size.

Note the Edit and Remove links shown in Figures 7.16 and 7.17. You can manage your listing using these two links to edit or remove it.

Clicking the Edit link opens the page shown in Figure 7.18, which is nearly identical to the page where you first created your listing.

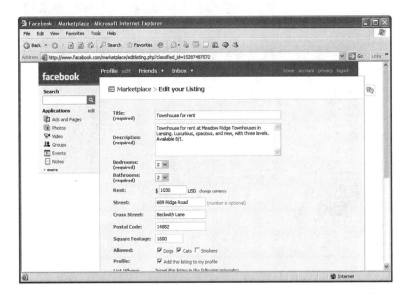

Figure 7.18
Editing a listing, top half.

It differs from the page where you first created the listing near the bottom, as shown in Figure 7.19.

As you can see in Figure 7.19, you can now add more photos to the ad by uploading them, and the button at the bottom now reads Update Listing.

One final note: a lot of spam appears in the Job listings. For example, people selling musical instruments to wannabe band members will target them by offering ersatz band gigs and tryouts. When you look at the listing, it's actually items for sale. You should probably avoid tactics like this. Although you might actually draw some prospective customers, your Facebook account will be short-lived. Here's what Facebook has to say on this point:

> "All Listings must be accurate and not misleading, and you may not use the Service in a fraudulent manner or to engage in any fraudulent activity or purpose or to impersonate any person or entity."

That takes care of listing items you're selling, but you might also want to list items you're looking for, as discussed next.

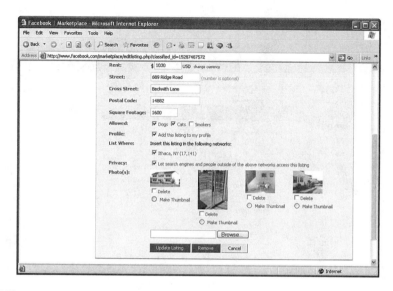

Figure 7.19
Editing a listing, bottom half.

Users Can List the Items They Want

Users can also advertise for the items they want, and you can sell those items to them. Users can create their own listing and post it in the Marketplace. To post a listing, they start in the Marketplace home, as shown in Figure 7.20.

Figure 7.20
The Marketplace home.

They can click the List what you want button, which opens the listing page shown in Figure 7.21.

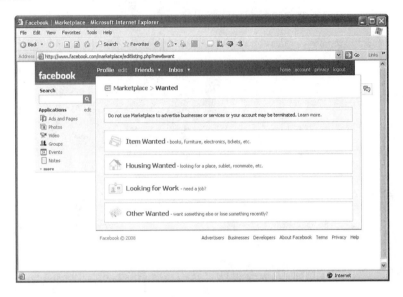

Figure 7.21
Creating a wanted listing.

Besides the usual warning to "Do not use Marketplace to advertise businesses or services or your account may be terminated.", these are the categories in Figure 7.21:

- Item Wanted - books, furniture, electronics, tickets, etc.

- Housing Wanted - looking for a place, sublet, roommate, etc.

- Looking for Work - need a job?

- Other Wanted - want something else or lose something recently?

Say you're a comics collector looking for a rare Walt Disney Bucky Bug comic from the 1920s or 1930s. In that case, you'd click the Item Wanted link, opening the page of sub-categories shown in Figure 7.22.

These are the available subcategories:

- Books - looking for a particular book?

- Furniture - looking for futons, beds, desks, tables, etc?

- Tickets - need tickets to a concert, sports games, etc?

- Electronics - in search of a particular gadget or computer?

- Cars - looking for a new or used cars?

- Other - looking for something else?

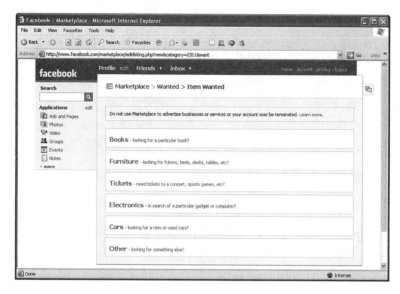

Figure 7.22

The wanted subcategories.

We're looking for a comic book, so click the Books item. This opens the page shown in Figure 7.23.

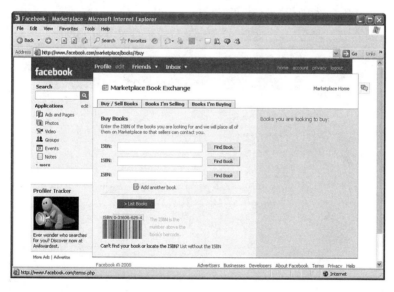

Figure 7.23

Looking for books.

Facebook asks for the book's ISBN. We can't list an ISBN for a 1923 comic book that we don't have. Click the "Can't find your book or locate the ISBN? List without the ISBN" link to open the page shown in Figure 7.24.

Figure 7.24
Describing the wanted book.

Fill in the details something like what you see in Figure 7.24, and click the Create Listing button. Facebook creates the listing, as shown in Figure 7.25.

Figure 7.25
Your new listing has been created.

To see your new listing, go to the Marketplace home and click the My Listings tab. You see your listings, as shown in Figure 7.26, complete with the listing for Bucky Bug comics. Not bad.

Figure 7.26
Your new listing.

Beacon, Polls, and Networks

In this chapter:

- Welcome to Beacon
- Understanding that Beacon is opt-in
- Working with polls
- Getting responses from polls
- Creating your own network

Introducing Beacon

As you know, the news feed is the most central aspect of marketing on Facebook. Through the news feed, your brand can spread virally with great speed, gaining thousands of fans a day. In fact, millions of fans have grouped around causes in three or four days this way.

Members' Facebook actions are posted to their friends' news feed. You plan to attend an event, and your friends know all about it. You post something new, and you can count on the word getting out automatically.

That's a very powerful marketing technique, and Facebook is aware of that. In fact, it's such a powerful technique that Facebook decided to share it with the world with a project named Beacon.

For example, say a Facebook member buys a book on Amazon.com. Don't you think Amazon would love to post a note about this in the news feeds of the member's friends? You can see the potential here. It takes the Facebook concept and distributes it throughout the Internet.

Advertisers loved the idea. Any Facebook member's actions on their site would be echoed to all their friends' news feeds. What a great marketing ploy! The Facebooking of the Web!

Users hated it. Perhaps you remember the firestorm of backlash that happened when Beacon was released in November 2007. Users felt their privacy had been invaded, and they took up arms against it with petitions and emails.

Mark Zuckerberg, the founder of Facebook, backed down on Beacon fast. This is how he put it in his blog on December 5, 2007 (http://blog.facebook.com/blog.php?post= 7584397130):

> "About a month ago, we released a new feature called Beacon to try to help people share information with their friends about things they do on the web. We've made a lot of mistakes building this feature, but we've made even more with how we've handled them. We simply did a bad job with this release, and I apologize for it. While I am disappointed with our mistakes, we appreciate all the feedback we have received from our users. I'd like to discuss what we have learned and how we have improved Beacon...."

Even now, a Google search for "Facebook Beacon privacy" yields 1,280,000 hits.

What Facebook did was to change Beacon from an opt-out program—where you had to specifically opt out if you didn't want to participate—to an opt-in program.

After the firestorm of disapproval, major advertisers backed away from Beacon, and things started to fall apart. What started as an apparent marketing triumph turned into a disaster. This is more evidence that if you push marketing too strongly on Facebook members, it will blow up in your face.

Beacon still exists (Figure 8.1 shows the page where Facebook explains it to potential advertisers), but it's a mere shadow of itself, and it remains largely an untested entity.

Now, if you're logged into Facebook and take some action on a Beacon affiliate's site, you have to explicitly approve the affiliate's posting an item to your mini-feed and news feed before it happens.

Facebook is also very clear that the affiliate site never gets any information about you, the Facebook user.

So, from marketing superstar to a mere shell of its former self, Beacon is all but moribund now. Some sites use it, but many Facebook users probably simply opt out.

Figure 8.1
Facebook Beacon.

What is the upshot for marketers? Beacon is now limited to a select set of large advertis-ers, and it's hard to get on the bandwagon. If you want to add Beacon support to your site, email beacon@facebook.com, but be prepared for a long wait to hear back.

Let's move on to Facebook polls.

Do any quotable pieces of wisdom for Facebook marketers come to mind?

Come on in. Put on your party hat and join the cocktail party. Keep it real & check the corporate-speak at the door. This is what you have to gain more professional and personal connections, more intel on your market, customers and competition, more fun and more profits—if you do it right.

Sherman Hu, creator and producer, WordpressTutorials.com

Introducing Facebook Polls

Facebook polls are great marketing tools because they let you interact with your poten-tial customers and get their opinions on various topics. For example, you might want to check how well a new product might be received, and a poll will tell you that.

This is an excellent technique for marketers, and it can be terrific fun watching the results come in. Imagine: instead of trying to puzzle out how to target your audience, you can actually ask them.

Polls are a powerful tool that give you an edge over actual bricks-and-mortar establishments, which can only watch as their customers drift in and out. Now you can talk to your potential customers and ask them what they want.

So many marketers struggle to figure out what their customers want. To many, their customers are simply a blank, unknowable Wall. So imagine what a delight it is to ask them specific questions and start getting immediate responses.

This is one way to conduct easy market research on Facebook. Your poll will appear in your target audience's news feeds as a text question with radio buttons for them to click, something like this:

Should you trust anyone over 30?

[ ] No

[ ] Yes

Note that polls can be only text-based at this time. No images or HTML are allowed.

All About Facebook Polls

Figure 8.2 shows the Facebook page that explains what polls are and how to start one. To get there, go to the Facebook business page at http://www.facebook.com/business and click the Polls tab in the upper right.

Targeting Your Poll

A good thing about polls is that you can target the audience you're questioning by

- Interests
- Location
- Age
- Sex

So you can target your audience. Note in particular that you can target your audience by location (that is, network) or by college, so if you're a marketer in a college town, you've got it made.

Creating and running a poll is simple. Let's give it a try.

Figure 8.2
All about Facebook polls.

Creating and Running a Poll

To create your own poll, click the Create a Facebook Poll button, shown in the upper right of Figure 8.2, which opens the page shown in Figure 8.3.

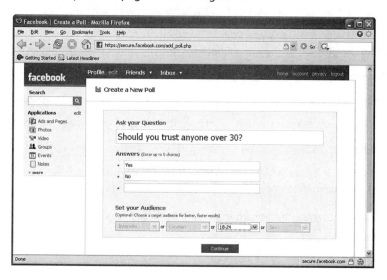

Figure 8.3
Creating a Facebook poll.

When you click the Continue button, the page shown in Figure 8.4 appears. On this page, you finalize your poll and arrange for payment.

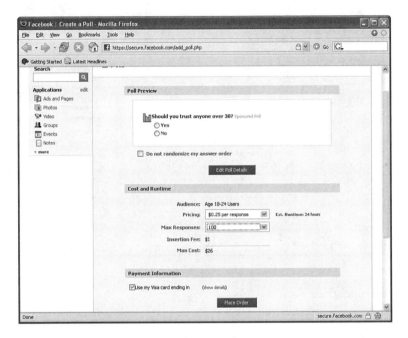

Figure 8.4
Paying for a Facebook poll.

You see a preview of your poll. It shows exactly how your poll will appear in the users' news feeds—a question, followed by two radio buttons with answers.

Facebook randomizes the answer order to avoid inherent bias, but you can change that by selecting the check box shown in Figure 8.4 directly under the poll preview.

- Audience: This is the demographic you've chosen. For us, that's 18-to-24-year-olds.

- Pricing: Here you set the price you want to pay, in terms of price per response.

- Max Responses: You set the maximum number of responses you want to pay for.

- Insertion Fee: Facebook usually charges a $1 "insertion fee" for each poll.

- Max Cost: This is Facebook's calculation of the most your poll will cost if you let it run until the maximum number of responses have been registered by users.

This page also shows the credit card that will be charged for the poll.

Click the Place Order button, and you're off. Facebook confirms that the poll has started, as shown in Figure 8.5. Facebook also sends you a confirming email.

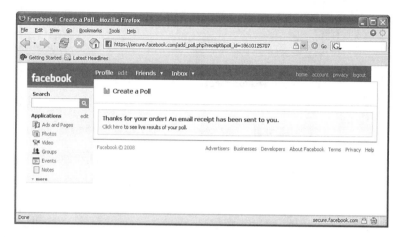

Figure 8.5
Your new poll has started.

Let's see how we did by monitoring our new poll.

> **What's the best way to get traffic to come to you?**
>
> There is no one best way to get traffic. It all depends on your outcome or intentions. In some cases, social media works. In others, blogging, podcasting, and video marketing does the job. And in other cases, paid advertising is the solution.
>
> My favorite combination of methods involve blogging, podcasting, video, and social media marketing.
>
> **Sherman Hu, creator and producer, WordpressTutorials.com**

Monitoring a Poll

Now your poll is running. We're asking 18-to-24-year-olds whether they can trust anyone over 30. How do you monitor the results?

You can click the "Click here to see live results of your poll" link shown in Figure 8.5, or navigate to the URL sent to you in the confirming email. Doing so opens the page shown in Figure 8.6.

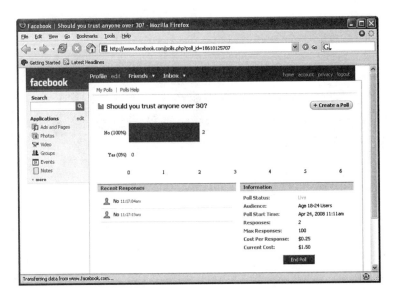

Figure 8.6
Monitoring a Facebook poll.

Figure 8.6 shows the results of the poll a few minutes after it has begun. As you can see, there are already a few responses. They're weighted heavily toward not trusting people over 30, which is not surprising, given the demographic we're polling.

Figure 8.7 shows the results about an hour into the poll. As you can see, the results are still heavily against trusting anyone over 30.

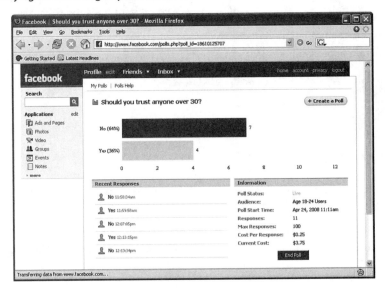

Figure 8.7
Monitoring a Facebook poll after an hour.

You don't have to click the Refresh button in your browser to update the displayed poll results. Facebook does this periodically.

After about an hour, I'm ready to terminate the poll (this is costing me money), so I click the End Poll button, shown in Figure 8.7.

Getting the Demographics of Your Poll Respondents

When you end the poll, or it ends by itself, you get a demographic report of the results, as shown in Figure 8.8.

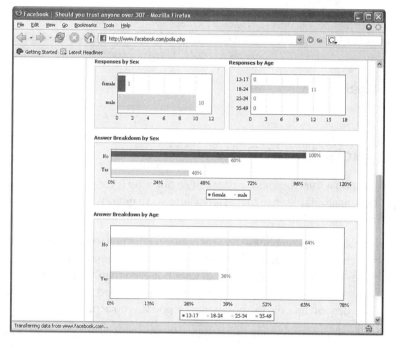

Figure 8.8
The demographic results of the poll.

As you can see, Facebook gives you a breakdown by the age and sex of your respondents.

So although you can select only a single audience-selection criterion when you start a poll, you get an additional breakdown when the poll ends.

Facebook also sends you an email when the poll ends or you end it; here's what that looks like in this case:

"Hi Steven,

"The Facebook Poll (order #25088411) you recently purchased has finished running!

"To see the final results, go to: http://www.facebook.com/polls.php?poll_id= 18610125707

"Responses Desired: 100

"Actual Responses Received: 11

"Price per Response: $0.25

"Your credit card *XXXXXXXXXXX* has been charged an additional $3.75

"This completes your order.

"To create another Facebook Poll, go to http://www.facebook.com/polls.php

"Thanks again,

"The Facebook team"

More Facts About Polls

Another question is, can you change or modify a poll after it's started? The answer is no. And it doesn't really make sense to do so, because you'll get results that are a mixture of the different versions of your poll.

When you create a poll, Facebook estimates how long the poll will take to reach the number of responses you requested. Obviously, it's just an estimate. In my experience, Facebook gives itself a generous amount of time, but even then, it sometimes comes up short with the number of responses it promised in the specified time. In such cases, Facebook charges you for only the number of responses you actually received.

Sometimes the opposite happens. Facebook underestimates the rate at which members will respond to a poll, and you end up with more responses than you asked for. That doesn't happen often, and Facebook charges you for only the number or responses you asked for, but it can be a little awkward.

Say you ask for 100 responses and get 111. To compare with other polls that got exactly 100 responses, which ones should you remove? Multiplying by a corrective factor isn't of much use, because you end up with fractional respondents. For example, if one answer got 47 votes, and you wanted to correct that to be able to compare the poll to other polls with 100 responses, you would have to correct by a factor of 100/111. This would mean that 47 votes for a particular answer would become 42.34. Try explaining that .34 of a vote during your boardroom talk.

If this becomes an issue, you can always stop your poll when the exact number of votes you want has been reached.

After you have your poll results, how do you go about quoting them? Facebook is very particular about this, because it has had problems in the past when poll results have been quoted as "According to Facebook, 83% of ... ." As you can see, that's an issue, because the source was a Facebook poll, not Facebook itself.

For that reason, Facebook asks that you source poll results something like this: "According to a survey conducted by XYZ on Facebook Polling, 80 percent of respondents ... ."

That concludes our study of Facebook polls. They're a useful way to keep in touch with your potential customers. Where else can you ask people questions about their preference and get responses in mere minutes?

As a marketer, it's a thrill to be able to hear from your potential customers. Too often, marketers end up thinking of their audience as a large, faceless, silent mass that must somehow be appeased and cajoled. With Facebook polls, your audience can talk to you, answering your questions ("Which would you rather own, an iPod or an iPhone?") and giving you needed data on how to target your efforts.

Still, you must be careful not to spam or give the appearance of spamming ("Have you seen our site at www.biggiebiz.com?"). If you spam the polls, Facebook will shut down your account.

Spam in general is not well tolerated on Facebook. This can be frustrating to marketers ("That's not spam! All I did was ask if anyone wanted to try to win free movie tickets!"). What's spam and what's not is usually up to the members. But it's their venue, so you have to fit your marketing efforts into it.

So of all the parts of Facebook, which tolerates what might be called spam the most? That would be network pages.

Using Facebook Network Pages

You already know about Facebook networks. They're those groupings of members by geographic region, workplace, college, or high school. What we haven't discussed yet is that all networks get their own page on which members can interact—and you can post marketing materials.

As with the rest of Facebook, spam here is still considered spam, and your account could be at risk if you create spam. But through the weight of multiple marketing efforts, what could be called spam in other parts of Facebook is tolerated on network pages the best.

Bear in mind that the marketing environment on Facebook changes continually. First Beacon was there, then it wasn't. First you couldn't display clickable ads, and then you could. First there were sponsored groups, and then they were replaced by pages.

Sponsored groups are still available on Facebook; we haven't discussed them yet for two reasons. First, they're being replaced in practice by Facebook pages. Second, they cost $100,000. If the price tag isn't enough to dissuade you, their declining popularity as they're being replaced by pages should.

We'll start our discussion about networks and network pages with an overview of joining networks.

Joining Networks

You can't join just any network. Again, Facebook is very protective of preserving a sense of community and keeping out spammers. Here are the Facebook rules as to which groups you can join:

> "To join a college network, you need to have a valid school email account. If you've already graduated, college alumni email accounts work too. You must be able to access this email address to confirm your affiliation. Join a college network from the 'Networks' tab of the Account page.

> "To join a high school network, you must be a current high school student. If you have a school email address or an invitation from another member of your high school network, you will be able to affiliate during registration. Alternatively, you can register for the site as an unaffiliated high school user. You will be asked to list your high school's name. Once you are on the site, you will need to be approved by a member of your high school network in order to join it. If you do not successfully affiliate with a high school network within sixty days, you will no longer be able to use the site.

> "To join a work network, you need to have a work email address from a supported company. This will put you on a network with your coworkers. Join a work network from the 'Networks' tab of the Account page.

> "To join a regional network, you simply have to let us know where you live on the 'Networks' tab of the Account page. Just enter your city, and we'll show you the regional networks closest to you. You cannot change regional networks frequently, so please be sure to pick the right one to join."

And take a look at this:

> "Also, please note that if you [change networks] to a school that you do not attend and are reported for doing so, you will be permanently banned from the site."

You can be a member of up to five, but no more than five, networks on Facebook at the same time.

Overall, the restricted access to networks can be a problem for marketers, unless you want to market only to a specific network. For example, you wouldn't necessarily market Meadow Ridge Townhouses in New York state to California residents.

Although the exclusivity of networks decreases spam, it also limits your ability to reach target audiences outside very specific work, school, or geographic networks. You can create your own networks (and you'll see how to do that soon), but you can't create "sponsored" networks around your business, as you can with pages or groups. Any new networks still have to be region-, school-, or workplace-oriented.

So how do you join a network you're eligible for? Click the Networks tab in the Account page, or go to http://www.facebook.com/editaccount.php?networks, as shown in Figure 8.9.

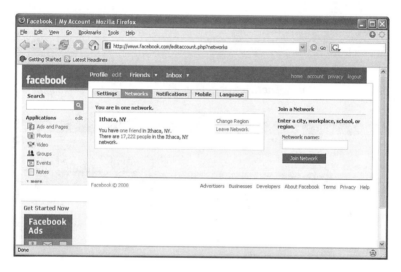

Figure 8.9
Joining a network.

How do you find a network to join? You can't really browse networks here, but you can start typing the name of one and see if Facebook recognizes it.

For example, you might type San Francisco, CA, which is a valid Facebook network, but you'll get a warning from Facebook similar to this, as shown in Figure 8.10:

> "You can only be in one regional network at a time. If you join the San Francisco, CA network, you will leave the Ithaca, NY network. You can only change regional networks twice every 60 days. Your last change was on Mar 26, 2008."

And if you try to join a workplace network, Facebook attempts to verify you by work email address, as shown in Figure 8.11.

Figure 8.10
You can be in only one regional network at a time.

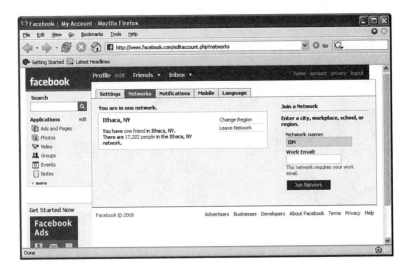

Figure 8.11
Joining a work network.

Let's say that you've signed up for all the networks you can, and you want to access the network pages. How do you do that?

Accessing Network Pages

You can take a look at the networks you belong to by going to your network page. My network page appears in Figures 8.12 and 8.13.

Figure 8.12
A network page, top half.

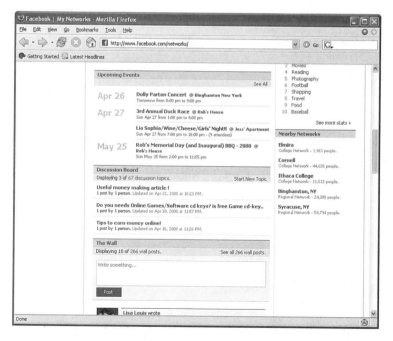

Figure 8.13
A network page, bottom half.

Here are the sections on this page:

- Network Info: Data on the network, which includes the following:
    - Members: 17,225
    - Friends: 1
    - Type: Regional
- People in Ithaca, NY: Believe it or not, all the people in the network are displayed—six at a time.
- Popular in Ithaca, NY: Posted items and groups popular with the people in the Ithaca, NY network.
    - Posted Items
    - Groups
- Marketplace: Marketplace items posted by people in the Ithaca, NY network.
- Network Statistics: More data about the network, listing the "Top Interests" of people in the network. These are the top interests for the Ithaca, NY network:
    1. Music
    2. Art
    3. Movies
    4. Reading
    5. Photography
    6. Football
    7. Shopping
    8. Travel
    9. Food
    10. Baseball
- Upcoming Events: Upcoming events that were created as part of the Ithaca, NY network.
- Discussion Board: The Discussion Board is always crammed with spam.
- Nearby Networks: A list of nearby networks you might be interested in:
    - Elmira
    - Cornell
    - Ithaca College
    - Binghamton, NY
    - Syracuse, NY
- The Wall: The Wall is Spam Central in network pages, as we'll discuss here.

You'll find the most spam in the Discussion Board and the Wall.

Figure 8.14 shows some of the Wall posts.

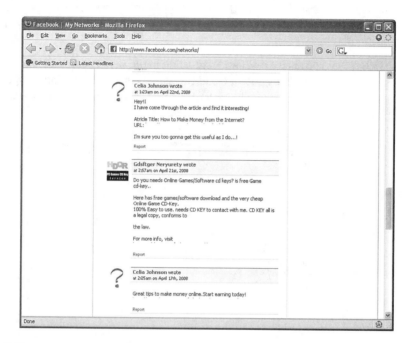

Figure 8.14

A network page with spam on the Wall.

So what are the upsides and downsides of posting on network pages?

Posting on Network Pages

There's always spam on the Wall and Discussion Board on Facebook network pages.

As you can see, some of these items are pure spam—and this is just about the only place where so much spam is tolerated on Facebook.

You can report the spam here. All you have to do is to click the Report link visible in Wall posts, or the Report link that appears when you open a Discussion Board post. But most people don't report the spam.

That's a double-edged sword. Although it means that you can post commercial messages here for free with more impunity than in the rest of Facebook, it also means that most users, tired of the spam, skip these sections.

So although you can post commercial messages more freely here than on other places in Facebook, they may just be ignored. Your mileage may vary, but I haven't found network pages to be terribly good for marketers—even those with legitimate posts.

In larger cities, there's so much spam that anything you have to say in the Discussion Board or the Wall gets scrolled off the screen rapidly.

So although you can try posting messages here, if the network page you're posting to is spammy (many workplace network pages are patrolled and the spam reported), be prepared to be ignored.

And don't forget that you're also restricted to posting in the networks you belong to. You can browse to other networks by entering a network name in the Browse other Networks box you see in Figure 8.12. For example, I'm looking at the San Francisco, CA network in Figure 8.15.

Figure 8.15
The San Francisco network page.

Although I can look at the San Francisco network page, I can't post anything to it because I'm not a member of the network—at least, not until I join it.

For example, take a look at the Discussion Board shown in Figure 8.15. There's no Start New Topic link, as there is for the Discussion Board in the Ithaca, NY network, because I am not a member of that network. Although I can open posts in the San Francisco Discussion Board, there are no Reply to *xxxxx* links as there are for the posts in the Ithaca, NY Discussion Board.

And when I look at the San Francisco Wall, there is no Write something... box as there is for the Wall on the Ithaca, NY network. All of this means that although you can often read the network pages of networks you don't belong to, you can't post on them. And that's probably a good idea from Facebook's point of view. If everyone could post on any network page, they'd all be choked with spam.

In my experience, users go to network pages to look at local events, as well as Marketplace items. They no longer really read the Discussion Board and Wall posts, unless they're in a network where those sections are patrolled by spam fighters.

How do events show up on network pages? The event must be either open or closed, and one of the event's admins must have clicked the Publicize option on the event pages. Also, you must be a member of the network to see events on high school, college, and work networks. On the other hand, events on regional networks are usually visible to nonmembers looking at the network page.

How about groups? The group must be open or closed. Also, one of the group's admins must have clicked the Publicize option on the group's pages. Note that if you're not a member of the network, only groups on college and regional networks (that are set to open or closed and whose admins check the Publicize option) are visible. Groups in work and high school networks are never visible to nonmembers.

Don't see a network you like? Create your own!

Creating Your Own Networks

Theoretically, you can create your own network on Facebook, although in practice the process doesn't seem to move very fast.

You can suggest a new network to Facebook by going to http://www.facebook.com/ help.php?suggest, as shown in Figure 8.16.

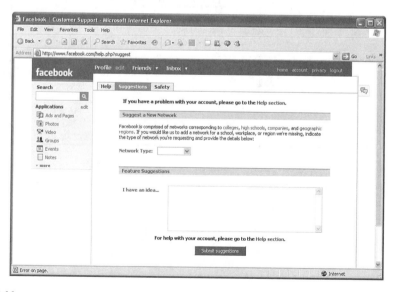

Figure 8.16
Suggesting a new network.

You start by specifying the type of network:

- High School
- College
- Work
- Region

If you select Work, you see these boxes, as shown in Figure 8.17:

- Company Name
- Company Email
- Company Website
- City/Town
- Your Contact Email

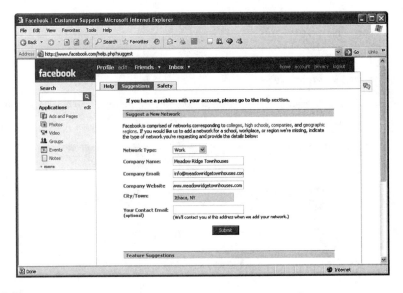

Figure 8.17
Suggesting a new work network.

After filling in the required info and clicking Submit, you see the results shown in
Figure 8.18.

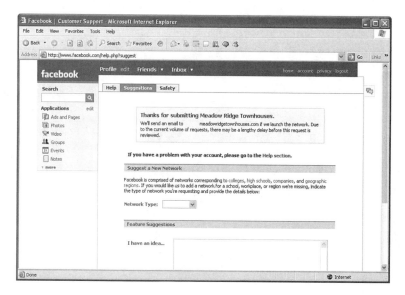

Figure 8.18
Having suggested a new work network.

Cool. Now you've suggested your own network. Note, however, that the odds seem
against Facebook's creating your new network unless you're a very large corporation. I
submitted that request for a new Meadow Ridge Townhouses network a long time ago,
and I never heard from Facebook about it.

Facebook Applications

In this chapter:

- Welcome to Facebook applications
- Advertising through applications
- Using applications to spread your network
- Creating your own application

Introducing Applications

Facebook is great, but you can probably think of ways to improve it. You might want to text-message your friends without leaving Facebook, for example. Or perhaps you want a space to draw graffiti on someone's profile. It turns out there's no end to the number of ways you can customize and augment Facebook with *applications*.

This chapter is all about Facebook applications—wildly popular bits of code you can embed in Facebook profiles and pages to augment Facebook. Originally starting off slowly, Facebook applications have taken off, getting hundreds of millions of uses every day.

Applications take over a small rectangular space in your profile or business page. You can use them to play games, connect with other users, look at clocks, monitor friends, play "lotteries," and more. The Facebook experience wouldn't be complete without a chapter or two on applications, because they've become so widespread. Some people go overboard and choke their profile page with a dozen or more. And there's no denying the fun factor.

But how can you, the marketer, profit from Facebook applications? There are at least four ways, depending on how involved you want to get.

Extend Your Contacts

Facebook is all about maintaining a web of connection between friends, and many applications—often the most popular ones—augment that process. Applications such as the popular iLike let friends connect, and there are ways to use that to promote yourself and your brand, as we'll discuss in this chapter.

Other applications let you extend the reach of your contacts. One application lets you display your LinkedIn business profile on Facebook, for example.

Other applications let you write directly to your mini-feed, send lists of people notifications, and even write to other people's news feeds (although most people I know who've used that application seem to have trouble getting it to work).

Extending your own web of contacts is clearly a good idea for marketers. Getting the word out is always a terrific idea. And Facebook applications can help, as we'll discuss in this chapter.

Advertise Using Prebuilt Applications

The fact that applications have become so popular has meant that advertisers haven't been far behind. Plenty of popular applications have been built to display advertising, and that's led to entire advertising networks.

And that means, in turn, that you can take out space on Facebook using those advertising networks. That's another avenue for your advertising on Facebook, and we'll take a look at using these networks in this chapter.

Advertising this way can be a good way to take advantage of applications. You don't have to develop your own applications from scratch, and you don't have to worry about being banned from Facebook, because the ad networks and the application developers take the risk.

This is one of the primary ways that application developers make money—by letting advertisers advertise through their applications. The more application installations they have, the larger an advertising base they have.

Have a Custom Application Developed

Besides using preexisting applications to spread the word about your brand, you can have a dedicated Facebook application created for you.

This is a great chance not only for dedicated advertising, but also to have the word spread virally about your brand. That's happened recently for several large corporations that had their own applications developed.

We'll take a look in this chapter at just how you go about having your own Facebook application developed. Some companies will do the work and make the new application available on Facebook for you.

Write Your Own Application

Finally, you can develop a Facebook application yourself. If you're a developer who wants to take the time to code your own solution, or a corporation with a team of developers, this can be a useful route to take. We'll take a look at this process—including some rules for application developers—in the next chapter.

This is the premier option if you can afford it. Creating your own popular application can be a big winner on Facebook—if it's popular. Some soft drink manufacturers, for example, have hit it really big with Facebook applications.

We'll start this chapter by looking at applications in general—what they are, what they can do, how to find them, how to install them, and how to uninstall them.

After that, we'll discuss how to leverage existing applications to your benefit, including using them to expand your web of contacts and advertise using applications. And we'll also look at how to get an application developed.

Any advice on branding your company on Facebook?

You don't need to plaster You, Inc. in Facebook. Think out of the box. Consider Dove's Campaign For Real Beauty.

Dove's campaign pushed forward a global effort to serve as a starting point for societal change and act as a catalyst for widening the definition and discussion of beauty. What about you and yours? What can you initiate in Facebook that will revolutionize and attract masses of Facebook users to champion a global cause, that you/your company sponsors?

Sherman Hu, creator and producer, WordpressTutorials.com

Finding Facebook Applications

Welcome to the wild world of Facebook applications. Not all applications are developed by third-party developers; some are developed by Facebook itself.

In fact, many of the built-in sections taken for granted in Facebook profiles are actually applications.

How do you find what applications are available?

Using the Facebook Application Directory

Facebook presents the applications it has available in the Application Directory, which is at http://www.facebook.com/apps/.

You can navigate to the directory by clicking either the Applications link on the left of all logged-in Facebook pages or the "edit" link next to the Applications link. Doing so opens the Edit My Applications page, shown in Figure 9.1.

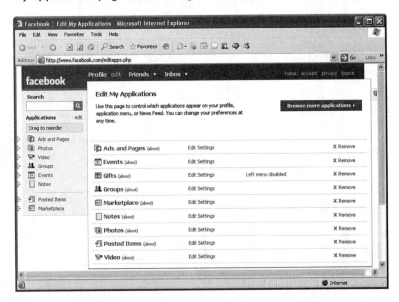

Figure 9.1
The Edit My Applications page.

To get to the Application Directory, click the Browse more applications button. Doing so opens the Application Directory, shown in Figure 9.2.

The Application Directory starts by displaying applications that can be installed in users' profiles. Note the tabs across the top of the page.

Figure 9.2

The Application Directory.

The Recently Popular tab displays the apps that have been the most popular recently, as shown in Figure 9.2. Clicking any of these takes you to the app's page. The Most Activity tab lists the apps with the most total uses. The Most Active Users tab takes you to the apps with the most dedicated users, who use these apps the most. The Newest tab takes you to the most recent apps.

Note that apps can be installed other places besides profiles, although the default is to show apps that can be installed in profiles. The links on the right in the Application Directory list other kinds of applications:

- For Facebook Profiles
- For Your Desktop
- For The Web
- For Facebook Pages
- By Facebook
- Apps You May Like

For example, clicking the For Facebook Pages link displays the applications you can install in Facebook pages, as shown in Figure 9.3.

Figure 9.3
The Application Directory, showing applications for pages.

Thousands of Facebook applications are available, so Facebook categorizes them, as you can see in Figure 9.2 for profile apps. Here's the list of categories:

- Alerts (1,028)
- All (22,925)
- Business (1,004)
- Chat (1,279)
- Classified (337)
- Dating (1,581)
- Education (1,728)
- Events (1,031)
- Fashion (673)
- File Sharing (217)
- Food and Drink (613)
- Gaming (2,655)
- Just for Fun (9,609)
- Messaging (1,326)
- Mobile (349)
- Money (388)
- Music (1,216)
- Photo (1,007)
- Politics (705)
- Sports (2,031)
- Travel (579)
- Utility (1,862)
- Video (977)

Clicking a category opens that category's page.

Suppose you've found an application you like, such as the popular Super Wall, shown in Figure 9.3. How do you get a better look at it?

Looking at an Application

Just click the listing for Super Wall, shown in Figure 9.3, to open the page for the application, shown in Figure 9.4.

Figure 9.4
The Super Wall page.

Super Wall shows you what the application looks like, along with a description ("Super Wall lets you send comments, photos, videos, graffiti, and more to friends!").

This application extends the normal Facebook Wall into something new, where you can write graffiti, post videos and photos, and the like. Super Wall is one of the more popular Facebook apps, with 2,171,274 daily active users, so let's add it to your profile now.

Adding an Application

Super Wall is one of those applications that you can add to profiles or pages. Note the buttons on the right of the Super Wall page—Add to Profile and Add to Page. Clicking the Add to Profile button opens the Add Super Wall to your Facebook account? page, shown in Figure 9.5.

Figure 9.5
The Add Super Wall? page.

Note the installation options you have here. You can let Super Wall:

- Know who I am and access my information: Granting access to information is required to add applications. If you are unwilling to grant access to your information, do not add this application.

- Put a box in my profile

- Place a link in my left-hand navigation

- Publish stories in my News Feed and Mini-Feed

- Place a link below the profile picture on any profile

- Send me notifications via email

Select the privacy options you want, and click the Add Super Wall button. Doing so brings up an important page for any application—the chance to get users to tell others about the app (see Figure 9.6).

The page shown in Figure 9.6 both welcomes you to Super Wall and lets you send "cards" to friends, telling them about Super Wall—thereby letting them add it as well.

Now that you've added the Super Wall application, you can see it in your profile, as shown in Figure 9.7.

Figure 9.6
The publicize Super Wall page.

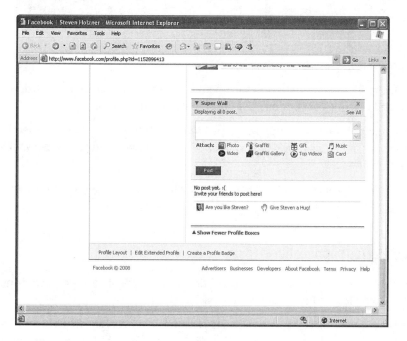

Figure 9.7
The Super Wall.

Now you can use the tools shown in Figure 9.7 to upload photos, draw and send graffiti, upload music, and so on. Cool.

For example, to post graffiti on your friends' Super Walls, click the Graffiti tool link shown in Figure 9.7. This opens the page shown in Figure 9.8.

Figure 9.8
Posting graffiti on your friends' Super Walls.

Select the friends you want to post the graffiti to, as shown in the upper right, draw your graffiti, and click the Post button. Your post is sent to your friends.

You can also post graffiti to your own Super Wall by selecting yourself in the friends box, drawing your graffiti, and clicking Post. Your new post shows up in your Super Wall, as shown in Figure 9.9.

So now you understand a fairly standard Facebook application—Super Wall. There's more to the story, however. You can also manage your applications.

Managing Your Applications

There are two ways to manage your applications—using the application's own pages, and managing it from Facebook's point of view.

To manage Super Wall using its own pages, click the Super Wall link that's been added to your list of links on the left of any logged-in Facebook page, which opens the Super Wall page. Click the Settings tab to open the page shown in Figure 9.10.

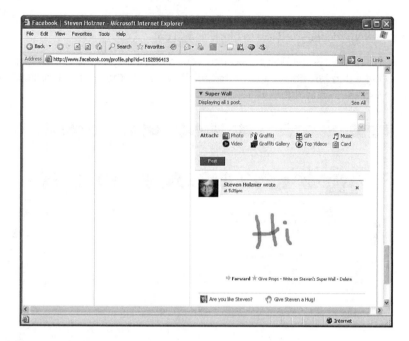

Figure 9.9
Posting graffiti on your own Super Wall.

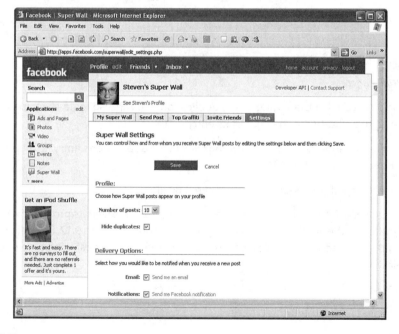

Figure 9.10
Super Wall settings.

On this page, you can configure Super Wall, setting the delivery options for posts, deciding which of your friends you'd like to block, and so on.

To manage the whole Super Wall application, you can click the Applications link on the left of any logged-in Facebook page, or the "edit" link next to the Applications link. This opens the page shown in Figure 9.11.

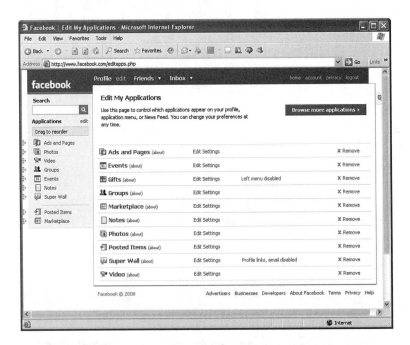

Figure 9.11
Super Wall pages.

This page lets you edit the setting of any application. You can also remove an application by clicking the X button to the right of its entry on this page.

To edit an application, click the Edit Settings link in the application's entry. This opens the dialog box shown in Figure 9.12.

So how many applications can you add? There's no limit.

The space in which the application appears in your profile is called its profile box. You can specify whether the application can display its profile box. In Figure 9.12, note the Profile Box setting at the top of the dialog box. You can set the profile box's visibility to one of the following:

- My Networks and Friends
- Friends of Friends Only
- Friends
- No one
- Customize...

Figure 9.12
Editing Super Wall settings.

If you don't want the profile box to appear, select the No one option. Note that even though not all applications have an actual profile box (the Facebook Events application does not have a profile box, for example), they all still display the Profile Box list box shown in Figure 9.12.

You can move your Super Wall to a different location on your profile. You can move any item in your profile if, when you move the mouse cursor over its light-blue title bar, a move icon appears. This icon is an up-down arrow if you can move the item up or down only, and it's a four-way arrow if you can move the item in any direction. If you see such an icon, just drag the item around as you like. Note that a user's Profile Picture, Basic Info, Personal Information, and Mini-Feed sections can never be moved.

You might also notice in Figure 9.12 that there's a check box labeled "Publish stories about this in my News Feed." Anything your friends do with applications appears in your news feed, and you can edit an application's News Feed settings by selecting or unselecting this check box.

Besides editing an application's settings, you can control applications through the Facebook privacy page, shown in Figure 9.13. To get there, click the "privacy" link at the top right of any Facebook page.

Privacy is a big issue on Facebook. When Facebook introduced the news feed, letting you see what your friends are up to, in just a few days a signed online petition asked Facebook to remove it.

Figure 9.13
Editing privacy settings.

Clicking the Applications link in Figure 9.13 opens the page shown in Figure 9.14. This page handles applications you've authorized to access your information. Because I haven't done that for any application here, the page is blank. Clicking the Other Applications tab opens the page shown in Figures 9.15 and 9.16.

Figure 9.14
Editing an application's privacy settings.

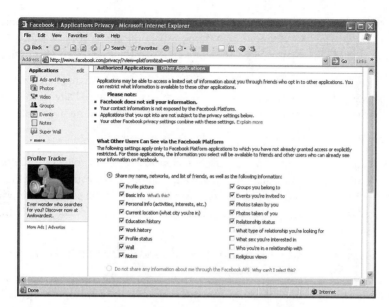

Figure 9.15
Editing an application's privacy settings, Other Applications tab, top half.

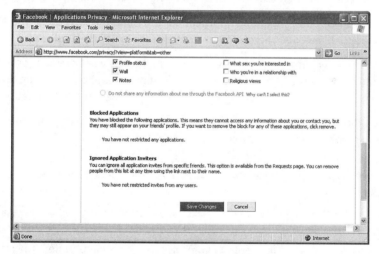

Figure 9.16
Editing an application's privacy settings, Other Applications tab, bottom half.

Note how careful Facebook is about reassuring users of their privacy:

- "Facebook does not sell your information.
- "Your contact information is not exposed by the Facebook Platform.
- "Applications that you opt into are not subject to the privacy settings below.
- "Your other Facebook privacy settings combine with these settings."

Note the extensive list of privacy items you can configure for Platform applications. The Facebook Platform lets developers create third-party applications, such as Super Wall. In Figure 9.15, you can let such applications share your name, networks, and list of friends.

You might also notice the "Do not share any information about me through the Facebook API" check box at the bottom of Figure 9.15. It's grayed out because I already have Super Wall, which uses the Facebook API (that is, the Facebook Platform) that is installed.

Here's what Facebook has to say about applications and privacy:

> "Applications built by third parties are not allowed to store or collect user information for any purpose. Basically, third party applications allow you and your friends to share information in cool and new ways, without affecting the security and privacy that you've always enjoyed on Facebook. This is an important privacy policy that Facebook takes extremely seriously."

But users' personal information can indeed be used and displayed by applications. What does Facebook have to say about that?

> "While third parties cannot collect user information for any personal purpose, applications will need to interact with user information to work on Facebook. In other words, Facebook applications will allow you to use your information in new ways to interact with your friends, while still maintaining all security and privacy."

Here's a final privacy note regarding applications. Applications can message you. How can you stop such messages, according to Facebook? Uninstall the application.

From a developer's point of view, it pays not to spam the user with messages or otherwise be obnoxious, because users can report your application to Facebook. They can do that simply by going to your application's page and clicking the Report this Application link.

Let's take a look at how you can use prebuilt applications for marketing purposes. The next chapter looks at developing your own applications.

What sneaky pieces of advice can you give? Something underhanded would work best here?

These two creative combinations of social media applications serve to save you time and duplicate your reach via syndication.

You can syndicate your blog's feed to your Facebook Notes application (the other application one can use is FlogBlog) and your Twitter account, so that whenever you publish to your blog, your Facebook and Twitter accounts are automatically updated, notifying your friends that you have something new on your blog.

You can also automatically update your Facebook status with every update of your Twitter account.

Sherman Hu, creator and producer, WordpressTutorials.com

Using Prebuilt Applications

Thousands of applications are available, already written and ready for you to leverage. Taking advantage of all that prewritten code is not only possible, but smart.

You can leverage prewritten applications as a marketer in two ways. First, many of these applications already installed on Facebook can display ads, and you can buy ad space on them. Second, you can use many of the prebuilt applications to expand your web of contacts on Facebook.

We'll look at advertising in prebuilt Facebook applications first.

Advertising in Prebuilt Facebook Applications

One of the ways that application developers make money is to allow their applications to show ads. Here are a few ad networks that let you advertise in Facebook applications:

- AdBrite (http://www.adbrite.com/mb/howitworks.php)
- SocialMedia (http://www.socialmedia.com)
- RockYou (http://www.rockyou.com)
- Adonomics (www.adonomics.com)
- Lookery (http://www.lookery.com)

Usually, ad networks have applications in place on Facebook—sometimes dozens of them. Ad networks use those applications to display ads for you and your brand.

For example, AdBrite is shown in Figure 9.17.

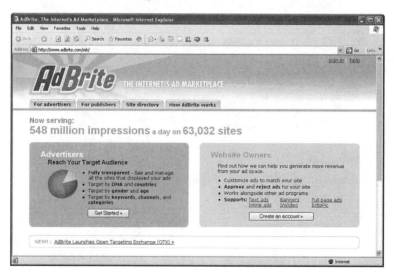

Figure 9.17
AdBrite.

Click the Site directory tab to see where AdBrite allows you to advertise, as shown in Figure 9.18.

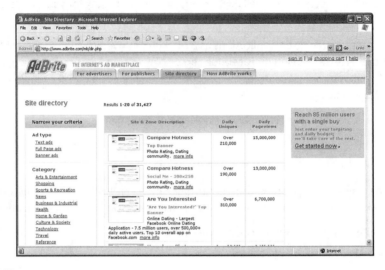

Figure 9.18
The AdBrite site directory.

The Are You Interested? application is a popular one on Facebook. When you click the "more info" link in Figure 9.18, you see what options AdBrite has available for advertising with that application, as shown in Figure 9.19.

Figure 9.19
Advertising on AdBrite.

You have two options—banner ads of 468×60 pixels, and text ads. To sign up, just click the Buy Ad link.

According to AdBrite, this application gets more than 310,000 unique users per day—not a bad customer base.

But who are those customers? Don't forget, one of the biggest advantages of marketing on Facebook is that you can select your target demographic. Clicking the Buy Ad link in AdBrite displays the window shown in Figure 9.20, asking you exactly what demographics you're interested in advertising to.

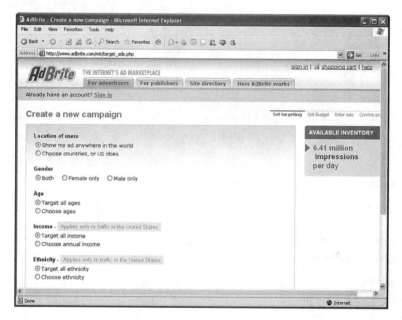

Figure 9.20
Selecting demographics on AdBrite.

As you can see, you can narrow the demographics of your ad pretty closely.

Or you might take a look at Lookery, shown in Figure 9.21.

With Lookery, you can select from a large number of apps. Here's how Lookery describes its mission with regards to Facebook applications:

"In July 2007, we launched a conventional display advertising network for Facebook applications, called Lookery for Facebook, because we kept hearing from people that they wanted to buy and/or publish traditional marketing campaigns in Facebook apps. We saw demand and went for it."

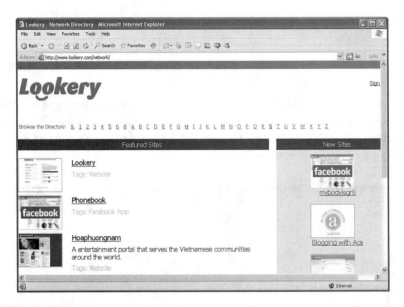

Figure 9.21
Lookery.

And here's a quote from an interview on SocialMedia's website:

> "Here's for an original name—SocialMedia Networks—which is a new ad network for—yes, social media sites. People spend a lot of time on social networks and they tend to be younger and quite Internet savvy. However, they are a fickle group who don't like overt marketing messages.

> "SocialMedia Networks says they're the first ad network to focus 100 percent on social media. They have over three billion ad impressions to more than 15 million unique visitors per month. These ad impressions are delivered within 5,000+ applications and they're appearing on Facebook, Bebo and MySpace."

Some sites also target application developers who want to get the word out on their applications. Here's a quote from the Rock You site:

> "Acquire 100,000 Users in One Day. RockYou's Ad Network is the cost effective method for rapidly acquiring users for your Facebook application. You only pay for results. New apps can acquire over 100K users in 24 hours and any app with full promotion can become a top 10 growing app. RockYou's Ad Network spans a suite of applications across multiple publishing partners adding over 500K new installs per day. Network applications include Likeness, Slideshows, X Me, Emote, Zombies, Horoscopes, Superwall, and more (all with over a million users)."

Gaining Exposure Through Apps

Another way Facebook applications can help you as a marketer is by spreading the word about you and your brand.

Let's take a look at a few such applications.

Super Mini Feed and Notifications

This useful application lets you write to your own mini-feed.

If you want a following on Facebook, it's important to keep an active flow of events going, and that's what this application can help you with. You can even post hyperlinks to your mini-feed, so people looking at your profile can click and go where you want to take them. Besides hyperlinks, you can post pictures to your mini-feed.

You can post up to 10 messages within a 48-hour time frame. And note that mini-feed posts can't be flagged as spam.

This application also lets you send notifications, and that's useful, but notifications *can* be marked as spam, so be careful about what you send. And this application lets you send up to 10 emails per day (as well as up to 40 notifications).

Super News Feed

This is an application that lets you post your own messages to your friends' news feeds— a marketer's dream. Being able to post to people's news feeds is a powerful technique, but you have to be careful not to come across as a spammer.

Regrettably, the only people I know of who've tried this application can't get it to work, and it currently has only one star out of five on Facebook.

iLike

The Facebook iLike application has been one of the biggies on Facebook. It lets users add music to their profiles using a music player.

More importantly from a marketing perspective, it lets bands publicize their music on their profiles, create their own iLike profiles, and dedicate music to Facebook friends.

When bands install iLike, they can create a Musician page, which provides more publicity for iLike users, in addition to their Facebook page. The band can upload images, videos of concerts, concert schedules, and, of course, music to their Musician page.

As a band, you can also dedicate your music to friends. Those friends receive the dedication and an optional message, which are automatically displayed on all their profiles. The music can be heard when the link is clicked. Not bad for publicity.

A band might even give a reward, such as free tickets, to people who dedicate the band's music to all their friends.

My LinkedIn Profile

Here's another network-building Facebook application. This one lets you link to your LinkedIn account from your Facebook profile.

Here's how My LinkedIn Profile describes itself:

> "Promote your LinkedIn account with a badge on your Facebook profile. Just enter your LinkedIn username or full url to your LinkedIn profile and choose the style of badge."

Sticky!

Is your Wall full of social back-and-forth? Is your discussion board clogged with spam? Are important messages to your target audience on your profile or page getting lost in the clutter?

If so, try Sticky!, which are yellow sticky notes for messages that you want to stand out. These are good for getting attention when the discussion board or Wall won't do anymore.

Blog RSS Feed Reader

If you have a blog that you want people to follow, consider this application. If you can tie your blog to an RSS feed, you can display those feeds on your profile, which directs people to your blog.

Here's what this application says about itself:

> "Publish multiple RSS Feeds on your profile. Blog RSS Feed Reader is a great way to drive traffic to your blog from your Facebook profile using a RSS Feed. Customise each RSS Feed with images, description and dates. The Best RSS Application on Facebook."

Plenty of other Facebook applications can foster networking and getting the word out. Browse what's available on the Facebook Application page.

Having Custom Apps Developed

Sometimes, nothing will do but having your own Facebook application. Some companies will create an application for you, such as Facebookster. The Facebookster site is at http://www.facebookster.com, and you can see it in Figure 9.22.

Figure 9.22
Facebookster.

Here's how Facebookster describes itself on its site:

> "Facebookster is a premier Facebook application and viral widget development company. We provide an end-to-end solution, designing, developing, deploying and scaling your application to millions of Facebook users. Our customers include Fortune 500 companies and leading technology and entertainment organizations."

Facebookster tells me that the average small-business application costs less than $1,000 and takes only about two weeks to develop.

There are other companies out there that will also will develop Facebook applications for you, including:

- Art & Logic (www.artlogic.com)

- Notice Technologies (www.noticetechnologies.com)

- Ayoka (www.ayokasystems.com)

- Invoke (http://www.invokemedia.com/facebook-and-social-network-application-developers/)

- Emerge (http://emergedgtl.com/widgets)

- Parnassus Group (http://parnassusgroup.com/category/facebook-services/)

However, tens of thousands of Facebook applications are all jostling for space. To get an appreciable number of users, yours has to be something special; it has to stand out and engage Facebook users. Otherwise, you'll be relegated to the realms of ignored applications. But if yours is a hit, there's nothing like it as far as marketing goes.

Developing Your Own Applications

In this chapter:

- Creating a new application
- Writing a JavaScript game
- Configuring an application
- Adding your new application to your profile
- Design tips

Creating a New Application

Maybe you want to create your own Facebook application, and you wonder if this would be difficult. At its most basic, you can just host your own application as a web page on your own website, written in whatever language you want, such as PHP. Facebook will give your application space in its own Profile Box in users' profiles.

To see how the process works, let's create our own Facebook application and get it running. To keep things simple, we'll write this sample application in JavaScript, and it will be a guessing game.

The idea is that to play, you guess a number from 1 to 10, and the game tells you if you're high or low—or if you got it.

Writing the Game

This game will be written in JavaScript and will have the title "The Guessing Game":

```
<h2>The Guessing Game</h2>
        .
        .
        .
```

We'll display a prompt to the users that says "Enter your guess (1 - 10):" and add a text field where users can enter their guesses:

```
<h2>The Guessing Game</h2>
Enter your guess (1 - 10): <input type=text id = 'guess' name = 'guess'>
        .
        .
        .
```

We'll add a button labeled "Guess" that the users can click to enter their guess. When the user clicks this button, the browser calls a JavaScript function named Guess:

```
<h2>The Guessing Game</h2>
Enter your guess (1 - 10): <input type=text id = 'guess' name = 'guess'>
<input type='button' onClick = 'Guess()' value = 'Guess'>
        .
        .
        .
```

We'll also add a button to let the user start a new game with a button labeled "New Game," which is connected to a JavaScript function named Begin:

```
<h2>The Guessing Game</h2>
Enter your guess (1 - 10): <input type=text id = 'guess' name = 'guess'>
<input type='button' onClick = 'Guess()' value = 'Guess'>
<br>
<br>
<input type='button' onClick = 'Begin()' value='New Game'>
```

All that remains is to write the Guess and Begin functions to make this game work. To do that, we'll add a JavaScript <script> element:

```
<script>
        .
        .
        .
</script>
```

```
<h2>The Guessing Game</h2>
Enter your guess (1 - 10): <input type=text id = 'guess' name = 'guess'>
<input type='button' onClick = 'Guess()' value = 'Guess'>
<br>
<br>
<input type='button' onClick = 'Begin()' value='New Game'>
```

Creating the `Begin` Function

We'll start with the `Begin` function. It creates a new answer that the user tries to guess. `Begin` stores the answer, a number from 1 to 10, in a variable named `answer` (which is outside any function, so it's accessible inside any function). The `Begin` function displays to the user an alert message box with the message "New game started. Try to guess the number!":

```
<script>
var answer;

function Begin()
{
  answer = 1 + Math.floor(Math.random() * 10);
  alert('New game started. Try to guess the number!');
}
</script>

<h2>The Guessing Game</h2>
Enter your guess (1 - 10): <input type=text id = 'guess' name = 'guess'>
<input type='button' onClick = 'Guess()' value = 'Guess'>
<br>
<br>
<input type='button' onClick = 'Begin()' value='New Game'>
```

Creating the `Guess` Function

When the user enters a guess and clicks the Guess button, the browser calls the `Guess` function. We start that function by reading the guess the user entered into the text field:

```
<script>
var answer;

function Guess()
{
  var guess = document.getElementById('guess').value;
       .
       .
       .
}
```

```
function Begin()
{
  answer = 1 + Math.floor(Math.random() * 10);
  alert('New game started. Try to guess the number!');
}
</script>

<h2>The Guessing Game</h2>
Enter your guess (1 - 10): <input type=text id = 'guess' name = 'guess'>
<input type='button' onClick = 'Guess()' value = 'Guess'>
<br>
<br>
<input type='button' onClick = 'Begin()' value='New Game'>
```

Now we have the user's guess in a variable named guess and the correct answer in a variable named answer. If the two are equal, we can display the message "You got it!" in an alert box, and start a new game by calling the Begin function:

```
<script>
var answer;

function Guess()
{
  var guess = document.getElementById('guess').value;
  if (guess == answer) {
      alert('You got it!');
      Begin();
  }
        .
        .
        .
}

function Begin()
{
  answer = 1 + Math.floor(Math.random() * 10);
  alert('New game started. Try to guess the number!');
}
</script>

<h2>The Guessing Game</h2>
Enter your guess (1 - 10): <input type=text id = 'guess' name = 'guess'>
<input type='button' onClick = 'Guess()' value = 'Guess'>
<br>
<br>
<input type='button' onClick = 'Begin()' value='New Game'>
```

On the other hand, if the guess was too high or too low, we can tell the user about it in an alert box and let him or her guess again:

```
<script>
var answer;

function Guess()
{
  var guess = document.getElementById('guess').value;
  if (guess == answer) {
      alert('You got it!');
      Begin();
  }
  if (guess > answer) {
    alert('Your guess was too high.');
  }
  else {
    alert('Your guess was too low.');
  }
}

function Begin()
{
  answer = 1 + Math.floor(Math.random() * 10);
  alert('New game started. Try to guess the number!');
}
</script>

<h2>The Guessing Game</h2>
Enter your guess (1 - 10): <input type=text id = 'guess' name = 'guess'>
<input type='button' onClick = 'Guess()' value = 'Guess'>
<br>
<br>
<input type='button' onClick = 'Begin()' value='New Game'>
```

Our game is complete. This game is written in JavaScript, but you could use other online languages, such as PHP. To make the game available as a Facebook application, we'll host it online so that it's accessible on the Web.

Testing the Game

After saving the game as game.html, now I upload it to a website, www.meadowridgetownhouses.com, to make it accessible from Facebook. That makes the UR of the new game http://www.meadowridgetownhouses.com/game.html. Figure 10.1 shows this new game at work.

As shown in Figure 10.1, you guess numbers, and the game tells you if you're high or low until you guess the answer. Cool.

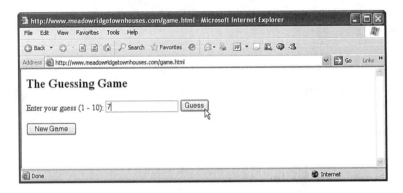

Figure 10.1
The new game.

Now let's turn our game into a Facebook application.

Any special advice on targeting specific markets that you may have been involved with (e.g., nonprofits)?

In serving both for-profits and non-profits, the practice is the same.

Research your market and topics in Facebook Groups. Preview the groups' activity, discussions, needs and wants. Join these groups. Add value with Q&A, photos, videos and discussions.

When you've added value, group members will click over to your Facebook Profile, which in turn leads them to your website/blog, and potentially increases the chances of them becoming a customer of your offerings. The end goal is to convert a Facebook member to be an evangelist of you, your company and your offerings, which repeats the cycle for other customers-to-be.

Sherman Hu, creator and producer, WordpressTutorials.com

Installing the Developer Facebook Application

To create a Facebook application, you have to use the Facebook Developer application. Yep, this is an application, just like any other Facebook application, but it lets you create Facebook applications.

To add the Developer application to your account, go to the Facebook Developer page, at http://developers.facebook.com/, as shown in Figure 10.2.

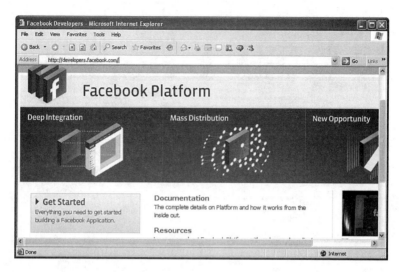

Figure 10.2
The Facebook Developer page.

Click the Get Started link, shown in Figure 10.2, to open the Get Started page, shown in Figure 10.3.

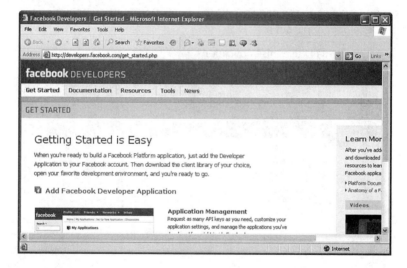

Figure 10.3
The Facebook Developer Get Started page.

Click the Add Facebook Developer Application link shown in Figure 10.3 to open the page shown in Figure 10.4.

This page gives you an overview of the Developer application. To add the Developer to your account, click the Add Developer button shown at the bottom of Figure 10.4.

Figure 10.4
Adding the Developer Application.

After a confirmation page, the page shown in Figure 10.5 appears, confirming that you've added the Developer application.

Now how do you actually use this application?

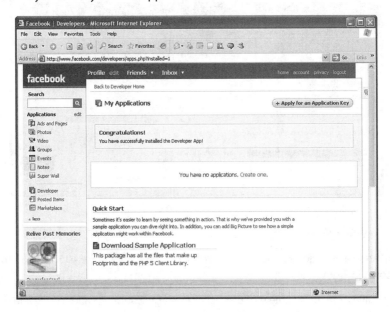

Figure 10.5
You've added the Developer application.

Using the Developer Application

To start the Developer application, click the Developer link that appears in the list of links on the left of any logged-in Facebook page. Doing so opens the Developer application, shown in Figure 10.6.

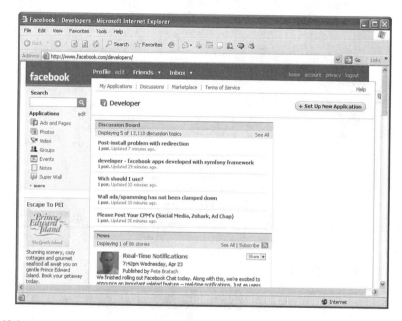

Figure 10.6
The Developer application.

The first step is to create a new application.

Converting the Game into a Facebook Application

You create a new Facebook application by clicking the Set Up New Application button, which you can see on the right of Figure 10.6.

To create the new application, you have to name and configure it so that Facebook can understand it. Clicking the Set Up New Application button opens the extensive configuration page shown in Figures 10.7, 10.8, and 10.9.

Filling out this form takes a little effort.

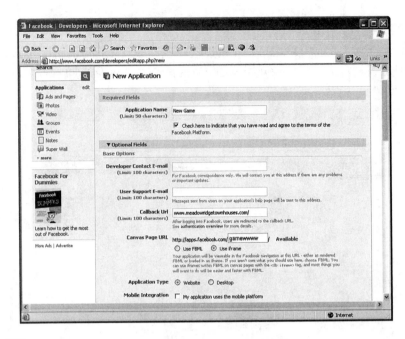

Figure 10.7
Setting up an application, top third.

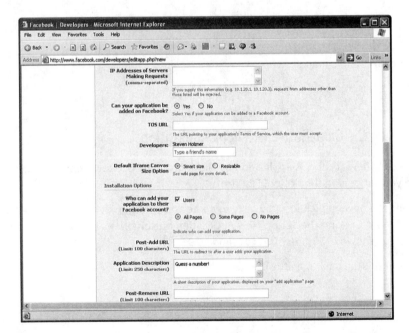

Figure 10.8
Setting up an application, middle third.

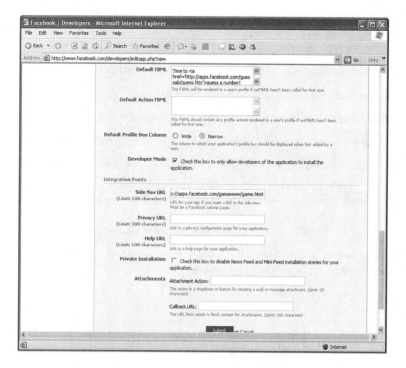

Figure 10.9
Setting up an application, bottom third.

Filling out the Application Configuration Form

The form shown in Figures 10.7, 10.8, and 10.9 has to be filled out correctly, or your application won't fly. Here's what the fields are, with the settings to use in this example shown in **bold**:

- Application Name: **New Game**

- Check here to indicate that you have read and agree to the terms of the Facebook Platform: **(Check this checkbox)**

- Developer Contact E-mail: **(Add your email here)**

- User Support E-mail: **(Add your email here)**

- Callback Url: This is the URL of the root directory of your application. In this case, it's **http://www.meadowridgetownhouses.com/**. Note that the final slash (/) is essential.

- Canvas Page Url: This is the name of a directory you want to host your application on Facebook. The canvas is where your application is drawn. Make up a name; don't use any numbers. Facebook Developer will tell you if the name is available, as shown in Figure 10.7. I used **gamewww** in this example.

- Use FBML or Use iframe: **Click Use iframe**.

- Application Type: Website or Desktop: **Click Website**.

- Mobile Integration: Select this if your application uses the mobile platform.

- Can your application be added on Facebook?: **Click Yes**.

- TOS URL: The URL pointing to your application's Terms of Service

- Developers: **Steven Holzner** (your name already appears in this text field)

- Default Iframe Canvas Size Option: The default canvas resizing option; leave this as it is.

- Who can add your application to their Facebook account?: **Click Users and then All Pages**.

- Post-Add URL: The URL to redirect to after a user adds your application.

- Application Description: A short description of your application, displayed on your "add application" page. I used **"Guess a number!"**

- Post-Remove URL: The URL at which you want to be notified when a user removes your application from his or her Facebook account.

- Default FBML: The default Facebook HTML (FBML) that appears in the profile box. I used "**Time to <a href='http://apps.facebook.com/gamewww/game.html'>guess a number!</a>**" in this example.

- Default Action FBML: This FBML should contain any profile actions rendered in a user's profile if set.

- Default Profile Box Column: **Select Narrow**.

- Developer Mode: Because we're only testing this application and not distributing it, **select the "Check this box to only allow developers of the application to install the application." check box**.

- Side Nav URL: This is the URL to your application's canvas that will appear in the list of links on the left of any logged-in Facebook page, as it would for any installed application. I used **http://apps.facebook.com/gamewww/game.html**.

- Privacy URL: The link to a privacy configuration page for your application.

- Help URL: The link to a help page for your application.

- Private Installation: Check this box to disable news feed and mini-feed installation stories for your application.

- Attachment Action: The action in a drop-down or button for creating a Wall or message attachment.

- Callback URL: The URL from which to fetch content for attachments.

After you've got all that filled out, click the Submit button at the bottom of this page. Your new application is created, as shown in Figure 10.10.

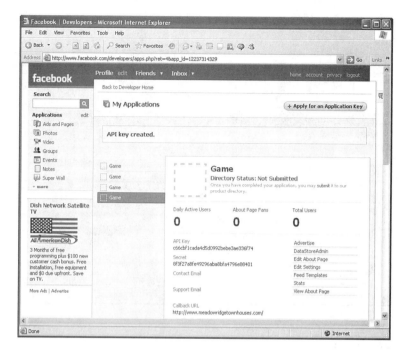

Figure 10.10
The created game.

Now let's install and test our new application.

Please give us the benefit of any additional wisdom that we didn't ask about?

You can effectively engage, educate and entertain viewers outside of Facebook with value-added videos (created using the video recording feature in your Facebook Fan Page), which will encourage them to join your Facebook Page. Through these videos, you can also direct them to your blog/website, or suggest a call-to-action for your offerings.

Many Facebook users or marketers do not know this, and you can be one of the few that will use this feature to generate new subscribers or customers.

Sherman Hu, creator and producer, WordpressTutorials.com

Installing and Testing the Game

To install the new application, go to its About page by clicking the View About Page link shown in Figure 10.10. This brings up the game's new page, as shown in Figure 10.11.

Note that because we haven't supplied an image for this sample game, you see a big question mark.

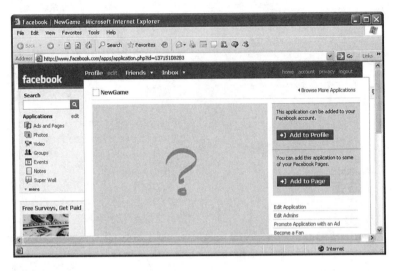

Figure 10.11
About the new game.

See the Add to Profile and Add to Page buttons shown in Figure 10.11. That's how you can add the new game to your profile and pages.

Click the Add to Profile button to open the new game (or you can start it with the New Game link on the left of any logged-in Facebook page), as shown in Figure 10.12.

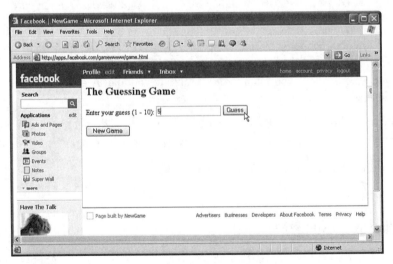

Figure 10.12
Playing the new game.

As you can see in Figure 10.12, the new game is functional in Facebook! Very cool.

You can reach your new game at any time by clicking the New Game link on the left of any logged-in Facebook page.

Note that the new application can't be distributed as a regular Facebook application until it has at least five friends.

That's the basic outline of creating a very simple Facebook application. However, this won't get you very far unless you write applications that can interact with Facebook. To do that, you need the Application Programming Interface (API).

Working with the Facebook API

When you create a new application, you get an API key and secret number, as shown in Figure 10.10. These values let your app connect to the Facebook API.

The API is a library of prewritten functions that your application can call to interact with Facebook, such as to get the current user's list of friends. You interact with Facebook through requests sent by your application, and each request includes your identifying API key and secret number.

You can download libraries of PHP or Java functions that you can call from your application at http://developers.facebook.com/resources.php, as shown in Figure 10.13.

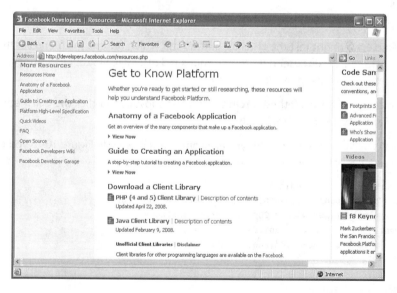

Figure 10.13
Downloading the API.

For example, if you click the PHP (4 and 5) Client Library link shown in Figure 10.13, you can download the PHP API library. You can configure it with your API key and secret number and place it in the same server directory as your application's code.

Want to test out the API functions? Take a look at the API test console, shown in Figure 10.14, which you can find at http://developers.facebook.com/tools.php?api.

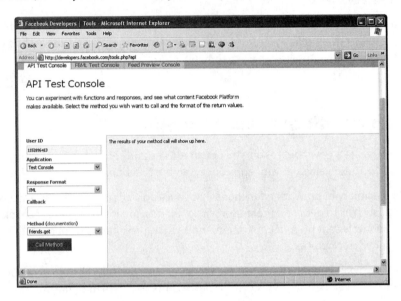

Figure 10.14
The API test console.

For example, we might test the `friends.get` API call, which returns the friends of the current user. I'm the current user here. My Facebook uid (user ID), 1152896413, appears in the API test console, as shown in Figure 10.14.

Select friends.get in the Method box in the API test console, and click the Call Method button. Figure 10.15 shows the results.

The results from the Facebook API typically come back in XML. In Figure 10.15 you can see the user IDs of my Facebook friends:

```
<?xml version="1.0" encoding="UTF-8"?>
<friends_get_response xmlns="http://api.facebook.com/1.0/"
xmlns:xsi="http://www.w3.org/2001/XMLSchema-instance"
xsi:schemaLocation="http://api.facebook.com/1.0/
http://api.facebook.com/1.0/facebook.xsd" list="true">
  <uid>712740</uid>
  <uid>1000564</uid>
  <uid>540680174</uid>
  <uid>553926276</uid>
  <uid>629356875</uid>
  <uid>650569027</uid>
```

```
<uid>656024475</uid>
<uid>1032555721</uid>
<uid>1046392211</uid>
</friends_get_response>
```

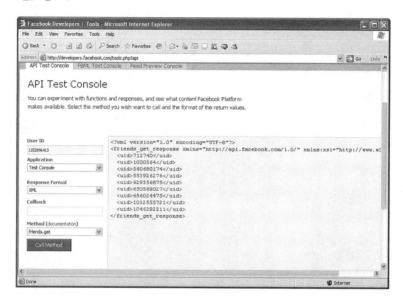

Figure 10.15
Using the API test console.

Cool. That kind of functionality is available to your application.

So you can get a person's friends as uids. How can you get more information on each friend? You can call `users.getInfo`, which gives an app just about all the information there is to know about a user (subject to his or her privacy settings, and Facebook has strict rules against storing this data).

You set the fields you want to read on any specific user. For example, `users.getInfo` recovers my first and last names when asked for my `first_name` and `last_name` fields, as shown in Figure 10.16.

Here's a partial list of the data your application can get on users with `users.getInfo`:

- `about_me`
- `activities`
- `college`
- `work`
- `birthday`
- `current_location`

- `city`
- `state`
- `country`
- `zip`
- `education_history`
- `first_name`

- `hometown_location`
- `interests`
- `last_name`
- `meeting_sex` (genders the person wants to meet)
- `movies`

- music
- pic
- political

- religion
- sex

- wall_count
- work_history

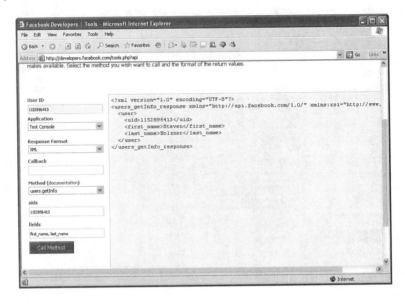

Figure 10.16
Using the API test console to find my name.

As you can see, any user who has set his privacy settings so that you can get access to his info is an open book to your application.

Your application stores its internal data in Facebook sessions, one session per user, so such information is preserved between page accesses. Sessions usually last 24 hours.

Applications have some limitations. By default, your application can make only 100,000 requests to Facebook in a 24-hour period (although you can increase that number by contacting Facebook). Here's Facebook's word on storing user data:

> "Any content delivered to the outside application can be safely displayed to the user. However, in general, content delivered when using a session key should only be stored until that session key expires. The exceptions to this are user ids and affiliations information."

What, in your experience, is the single most important topic or technique to know about Facebook marketing?

When creating applications, it is vital to make comprehensive use of all available viral communication channels, customizing your strategy according to your product for each one. Taking into account each channel, craft product scenarios that solve user communication needs in a very simple and straightforward way. This will provide more value to users and simplify your task as an application marketer.

Justin Smith, Editor, InsideFacebook.com, the first blog devoted to Facebook and the Facebook Platform

Facebook and Developers

The relationship Facebook has with developers has been evolving in an interesting way. After throwing open the floodgates to third-party developers, Facebook has indeed been providing more services for developers. The Developer Desktop, for example, now offers more analytics on things like your app's conversion rate (the ratio of users who add your app compared to the number who are invited to). But Facebook's main efforts these days seem to be focused on cracking down on spam.

Facebook gives all public applications a "spaminess" index; that index sets the privileges your application enjoys. For example, if your application sends out emails to users and you have a high spaminess index, the disable link in your email appears at the top of the email. But if you have a low spaminess index, the same button appears at the bottom of the email.

As an application developer, you do have to monitor Facebook's continual crackdown on spam and balance your efforts to spread the word about your application with what's tolerated.

For example, probably the most powerful way to spread the word about your app is through the news feed, which your application can write items to. In January 2008, Facebook changed the kinds of items you can publish. If such items contain links to application pages that require the user to add your application before they can be viewed, Facebook lowers the rank of your news feed's item.

Another thing application developers were doing was requiring users to invite friends before getting access to some of the app's functionality. Facebook jumped on that, turning off any app's ability to invite other users if it was guilty of that abuse.

It used to be that applications were limited to sending a maximum of 20 invitations per day, but that changed in February 2008. Now your application's invitation limit depends on its spaminess index, as determined by Facebook.

Notifications also have recently suffered a crackdown—to the point that many application developers avoid notifications altogether to avoid boosting their spaminess index.

Nonetheless, Facebook's efforts to curtail spam shouldn't inhibit your efforts to publicize your application. You can use ads, of course, but it's still true that the most powerful mechanism for spreading applications virally is the profile box (followed by the news feed). And, perhaps surprisingly, the Applications Directory is also a very popular way for users to find your application.

So design great graphics into your application—and keep it simple and engaging. Make your application something that users will want to invite their friends to use.

Index

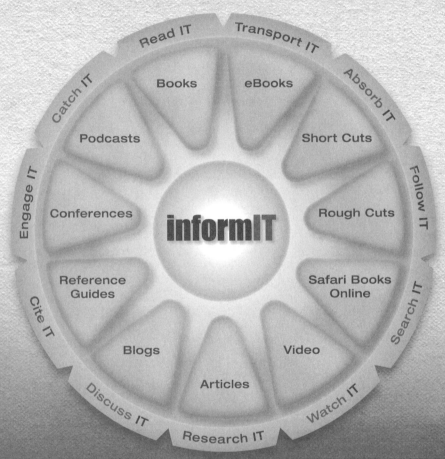

Steven Holzner

Facebook
Leverage Social Media to Grow Your Business
Marketing

FREE Online Edition

Your purchase of **Facebook Marketing: Leverage Social Media to Grow Your Business** includes access to a free online edition for 45 days through the Safari Books Online subscription service. Nearly every Que book is available online through Safari Books Online, along with over 5,000 other technical books and videos from publishers such as Addison-Wesley Professional, Cisco Press, Exam Cram, IBM Press, O'Reilly, Prentice Hall, and Sams.

SAFARI BOOKS ONLINE allows you to search for a specific answer, cut and paste code, download chapters, and stay current with emerging technologies.

Activate your FREE Online Edition at www.informit.com/safarifree

> **STEP 1:** Enter the coupon code: AGQZSAA.

> **STEP 2:** New Safari users, complete the brief registration form.
> Safari subscribers, just login.

If you have difficulty registering on Safari or accessing the online edition, please e-mail customer-service@safaribooksonline.com